082FCANF

D1333057

'AND I QUOTE ...'

and I quote...

a history of
using other
people's
words

ELIZABETH
KNOWLES

OXFORD
UNIVERSITY PRESS

OXFORD
UNIVERSITY PRESS

Great Clarendon Street, Oxford, OX2 6DP,
United Kingdom

Oxford University Press is a department of the University of Oxford.
It furthers the University's objective of excellence in research, scholarship,
and education by publishing worldwide. Oxford is a registered trade mark of
Oxford University Press in the UK and in certain other countries

First Edition published in 2018

Impression: 1

Published in the United States of America by Oxford University Press
198 Madison Avenue, New York, NY 10016, United States of America

British Library Cataloguing in Publication Data

Data available

Library of Congress Control Number: 2017959955

ISBN 978-0-19-876675-9

Printed and bound in Great Britain by
Clays Ltd, Elcograf S.p.A.

PREFACE

The genesis of the book has been my experience of working with quotations, especially in my role as Editor of the *Oxford Dictionary of Quotations*. My professional life as a historical lexicographer began as a library researcher for the *OED Supplement*, using the resources of the Bodleian library to search for earlier (and sometimes later) instances of words and phrases under consideration for inclusion in the *Supplement*. When subsequently I began to work specifically with quotations, I realized that the techniques needed to research and understand the way in which words and phrases develop in the language were also appropriate to understanding what can happen when a quotation becomes part of the personal or public vocabulary. Many quotations have their own 'stories', and these stories in turn illuminate the ways in which (consciously or unconsciously) we may quote. In this book I have focused particularly on quotations being used today, and many of my selections are taken from items encountered in the course of my work as an editor—most recently, for the eighth edition of the *Dictionary* (published 2014).

An essential feature of this book will be tracking in detail the language history of individual quotations through specific case studies. We all have an individual 'vocabulary' of quotations: it is likely that in many cases readers will have their own examples to illustrate the general points made, but I hope that this will only add to the interest of following selected stories. The instances in this book have in the main presented themselves through usage evidence and my own work on *ODQ*. The choice has been a personal one: something specific about a particular item has caught my attention. A different person might make a different choice, but I hope he or she would recognize the principles on which my choice was made to be valid. And, undoubtedly, for a future book I would make some different selections: the world of quotations constantly updates itself, and there is always another trail to follow, and another story to unpack.

ELIZABETH KNOWLES

Oxford
March 2018

ACKNOWLEDGEMENTS

In writing 'And I Quote ...' I have drawn on the work of fellow lexicographers at Oxford University Press. I am particularly grateful to my former colleagues Susan Ratcliffe, whose work has contributed so much over the years to the excellence of the *Oxford Dictionary of Quotations*, and Ben Harris, who generously read and commented on earlier versions of the text. I have learned a great deal about quotations by having the privilege of working with outside editors and consultants for Oxford Quotations dictionaries, especially the late Sir Antony Jay, Peter Kemp, and Lord Hennessy of Nympsfield. My editors at OUP have been supportive and encouraging.

It has been extremely enjoyable to work on this book, retracing and discovering individual quotation stories, and I hope I have been able to share some of that pleasure with my readers.

Material from the Oxford University Press Archives appears with the permission of the Secretary to the Delegates. Material in Chapters 6 and 8 that has previously appeared in *Dictionaries: Journal of the Dictionary Society of North America* appears with the permission of the Society.

CONTENTS

LIST OF FIGURES

INTRODUCTION

quotation, n. 5a A passage quoted from a book, speech, or other source; (in modern use *esp.*) a frequently quoted passage of this nature.

(*Oxford English Dictionary*, 3rd edn; entry updated June 2008)

Despite the certainty of the *OED*'s definition, 'quotation' can be a fluid term, as a number of studies attest.[1] In its widest sense, it may denote recognition of a formula that has been coined by another speaker or writer. It can cover a wide range of material, from a formally introduced and fully sourced extract to an unacknowledged (and possibly unrecognized) borrowing. It may also be used more loosely, to designate an idiom or saying. As Ruth Finnegan has shown (Finnegan 2011), 'quotation' is sometimes used to include both family sayings such as 'When in doubt tell the truth' and 'Don't expect life to be fair', and established phrases and idioms, such as 'as poor as a church mouse'. However, 'quotation' in terms of the *Oxford Dictionary of Quotations*, and as used in this book, represents an individual expression, in speech or writing, coined by a particular person at a particular time, even though we may now not know the details of authorship or first source. As such it differs from the broad stock of proverbs and sayings, which represent common wisdom, and the range of idiomatic phrases that have developed in the language from specific quotations. No boundaries are absolute: an established quotation may develop virtual proverbial status, or give rise to a related phrase. One of the purposes of this book is to examine the way in which this form of development takes place, and explore the links that can be traced between individual items.

Quotations are part of the fabric of the language. We are often highly conscious of them: coverage of significant events and people is frequently marked by a clustering of related quotations, often from diverse sources. The most 'successful' quotations, which have a demonstrable longevity and are still with us today, are those that were originally unique to a particular time, place, or person (real or fictional), but that have a quality of universality that means that they can offer the perfect expression in response to another place, person, or circumstance. Frequently, of course, they may be used in a sense differing from their original context, or be subject to wordplay or natural processes of language change in which one or more vocabulary items may be changed or replaced. Such developments are often a core part of a quotation's 'usage history'—that is, the record of how, in what contexts, and in what form, a particular item has been quoted through a significant chronological period of years. (The concept of currency through a timeline is not always straightforward—today an Internet search for a particular string may retrieve the digitized version of a nineteenth- or twentieth-century text along with contemporary uses. How readily, in such circumstances, will older sources be distinguished by the reader?)

In some instances, the originator will turn out to be a major literary figure, whose works have been widely read over decades or centuries. Pope is a substantial example; similar names might include Shakespeare, Milton, Jane Austen, and Charles Dickens. Their works have been widely disseminated, they are seen as figures of substance, and quotations from their material permeate the language. In April 2016, the *Washington Post* celebrated the return of *Game of Thrones* in its sixth season by challenging four teams made up of two reporters to guess whether given quotations were from a character in *Game of Thrones*, or a presidential candidate. (No one got all the answers right.) 'Canonical' figures may also include those who are seen as providing a particular moral authority: for example, a politician who, like Abraham Lincoln, is admired for his achievements.

Other well-established items have what might have appeared at the time a much more transient origin. When Mandy Rice-Davies died in December 2014, obituaries and accounts of her life included the information that her reported response 'He would, wouldn't he?' to being told that Lord Astor denied her allegations about his house parties at Cliveden had gained her entry into the *Oxford Dictionary of Quotations*. Related correspondence disagreed on whether she had actually uttered the words, or if they could be said to be a coinage, but there was a consensus that the quotation was a point of key interest (see Figure 1).[2] The *Observer* leader of 21 December 2014 referred to the phrase as words that had lived on through the decade because they 'captured a seismic and irreversible shift in the cultural and political mood'. More recently, the journalist Nick Cohen employed it in an examination of the presidential campaign of Donald Trump in America and the Brexit 'Leave' campaign in Britain. Noting how in both instances the operation of sinister forces was being adduced with some success, he commented: 'Everyone echoes Mandy Rice-Davies's line—"He would, wouldn't he?"'[3]

Figure 1. Mandy Rice-Davies arriving at the trial of Stephen Ward; her riposte, 'He would, wouldn't he?' at the committal proceedings remains one of the best-known quotations of the 1960s.

Quotations in written or spoken language may be heralded by such words as 'famously said', 'in the well-known words of', 'iconic words', and 'to quote X'. However, 'famous' in this context can be a highly subjective judgement, and mean little more than that it is well known to (and perhaps valued by) the speaker. Or it may simply have been employed to add emphasis to what is being quoted. A search for any of these strings will bring up a diverse collection of major historical figures, people associated with a particular event (of local or national interest), present-day celebrities, and fictional characters, together with established or supposed 'wise sayings' or proverbs. The 'quotations' cited may be authentic or apocryphal.

At the other end of the spectrum, there are quotations that have become so embedded in the language as vocabulary items that they are scarcely recognized as quotations—for example, phrases from

Shakespeare and the Bible. That said, as familiarity with the Authorized Version decreases, it is less likely that key phrases will be recognized as being 'from the Bible'. To take one instance, 'now we see through a glass, darkly' (1 Corinthians 13:12) in the King James Bible is represented in the popular *New International Version* translation as 'now we see but a poor reflection, as in a mirror'. 'Through a glass, darkly' is current as a phrase in the language today, but to what extent in the future will its biblical origins be recognized? ('Mirror' for 'glass' is not too great a difference—a contrast with modern versions of what the Authorized Version (Judges 5:25) designates 'butter in a lordly dish', which have virtually no point of contact with the seventeenth-century translation.)

In the middle there is a broad swathe of material in which particular quotations and sources rise and fall in favour, or gain new resonance through a change in events. Bismarck's comment in 1876 that German involvement in the Balkan conflict would not be 'worth the healthy bones of a single Pomeranian grenadier' was referenced widely in and between the two world wars.[4] It was reworked notably by Air Force Marshal Arthur 'Bomber' Harris in 1945, defending what even then was the controversial continued strategy of bombing German cities: 'I would not regard the whole of the remaining cities of Germany as worth the bones of one British grenadier.'[5] In the second half of the twentieth century it was more likely to be quoted in relation to historical accounts of Bismarck, but it surfaced pertinently in the House of Commons in 1995 in a debate on the role of the UN forces in Bosnia and is clearly still with us today.[6] To take one recent example, the *San Francisco Chronicle* of May 2015, covering the Victory in Europe commemoration parade in Moscow and considering Russian involvement in Ukraine, commented: 'So far both western Europe, which put security behind commercialism, and the war-weary United States have concluded that "Ukraine is not worth the bones of a single NATO grenadier" (to paraphrase Bismarck) and have rightly eschewed war as a solution.'[7] In another echo from the 1870s, reactions to terrorist attacks in Paris in November 2015 highlighted significant quotations from the time of the siege of Paris in 1870 ('Paris est la ville sacrée [Paris is the sacred city]'—Victor Hugo).

Significant anniversaries shed light on quotations associated with an event. In February 2016, the journalist Fintan O'Toole, writing in the *Guardian* about the Easter Rising of 1916 and the effect it had, entitled his column 'The Terrible Beauty of the Easter Rising Remains Alive Today'.[8] An exhibition on the Easter Rising that opened in the Athlone Library, Westmeath, on 10 February 2016 was titled 'A Terrible Beauty is Born'.[9] The Irish sportswear manufacturer O'Neill's, announcing its commemorative green jersey for 1916, carried on its website the inset quotation: 'All changed, changed utterly: A terrible beauty is born.' All these references are likely to be immediately understood as referring to the refrain of William Butler Yeats's poem 'Easter 1916', as would the title of Roy Foster's 2015 account of the Easter Rising, *Vivid Faces*. ('I have met them at close of day, coming with vivid faces.') While these are highly resonant quotations for this anniversary, they still tend to be used in a more literary context than another quotation of the time: 'Ireland unfree shall never be at peace.' This assertion now appears widely on memorabilia.

A change in the last few years has been the rate at which an utterance that has caught the public attention can be disseminated around the globe, achieving a level of instant recognition. A recent development of this process has been the quotation as hashtag—for example, as in *#JeSuisParis*. Social media can be used to find and discuss quotations—for example, what are regarded as inspirational quotes for a particular field of activity. It can, of course, also be a prolific source of misquotation. To quote the writer Jessica Valenti in the title of a column published in April 2016: 'On the Internet, you can never be quite sure who said what.'[10] Mistaken or fabricated attributions can be rapidly retweeted. On the other hand, wrong attributions can be highlighted very publicly.

An obituary published in 2009 highlights the contrast with an earlier time. In 1975, Rose Davis fronted a public campaign against the conviction of her husband George for armed robbery, making use of slogans through those means of publicity available at the time. As her *Telegraph* obituary put it: 'The case spawned a rash of graffiti around Britain—"George Davis Is Innocent OK" and "Free George Davis"—some of which still survive on walls and motorway bridges' (see Figure 2).[11] The campaign was very effective at

Figure 2. 1970s graffito with the slogan 'George Davis is innocent OK'.

the time, and Davis was released from prison, although his conviction was not formally quashed. In May 2011 the Appeal Court ruled that the conviction had indeed been unsafe, reported by the *Express* under the headline: 'OK, George Davis IS Innocent (but it has Taken 36 Years).'[12] The *Express* and other papers reflected on the successful graffiti campaign, a number of them carrying pictures. The BBC report noted that T-shirts and buttons had also been a feature of the campaign. In short, the publicizing of key slogans was done effectively through the means available in the 1970s and 1980s—which required creation and dissemination of a visual image to back up news reports and headlines. The instant global access of social media would, at that time, have been unimaginable.

The summer of 2016 provided some instructive instances of quotation use, from the citation of classic sources to the repetition of twenty-first-century utterances. One of the most difficult things in the world of quotations is to predict which new contenders will last. However, when the Chilcot Report on the Iraq War was published on 6 July 2016, one quotation was highlighted in virtually every account of the massive document in which it appeared. This was the assurance given by Tony Blair to George W. Bush, in a handwritten memo of 28 July 2002 eight months prior to the invasion, that 'I will be with you, whatever'. The text, as was pointed out by Mr Blair himself at a press conference on the day of publication in 2016, continued with the caveat, 'but this is the moment to assess bluntly the difficulties', and went on to contrast the situation adversely with Kosovo and Afghanistan. 'It is not even the Gulf War.' However, even in the immediate accounts it is clearly the first six words that embedded themselves in the public consciousness, and, while it is risky to prophesy, it seems likely that the impression will be a lasting one. Since the memo was actually written in 2002, the interest generated since its declassification in 2016 suggests that it has already withstood a certain test of time. All the key elements are there: the words are associated with a significant event, and have already been interpreted as reflecting a key relationship between two high-profile figures.

Some of what we quote is taken from our own experience: we repeat what we have read or heard. But since the eighteenth century, further help has been available through a wide range of published collections of quotations. Originally, of course, these were print sources, but today significant online resources are available to us at the click of a mouse. Some are intended to provide quotations that a reader can use. The *BrainyQuote* site says of itself: 'Whether it's a great quote for a birthday card, love letter, research paper or just for fun, BrainyQuote makes it easy to find great quotes.' Others are focused on validating attributions. *Quote Investigator* provides access to ongoing investigatory work related to 'who really said what?' Readers are encouraged to contribute both questions and answers, sharing what they have discovered, so that 'approximate solutions' are 'iteratively improved over time'. This, of course, has the huge advantage over a print dictionary of being able to provide a view of work in progress with the most recent updates, untrammelled by restrictions of extent.

Beyond this, direct self-help is now available for someone interested in how a quotation has been used over the years to search for it. Many works by major authors are now electronically searchable, allowing the reader to test whether (for example) the Cardinal de Retz is quoted by David Hume or Adam Smith. The 'Advanced Search' facility provided by Google Books allows you to filter a search for a string or group of words by date. Linked to this,

Google Books Ngram Viewer

Graph these comma-separated phrases: better angels of our nature   ☐ case-insensitive

between 1800 and 2000 from the corpus English ▼ with smoothing of 3 ▼   Search lots of books

(click on line/label for focus)

better angels
of our nature

G+ Share
Tweet

Embed Chart

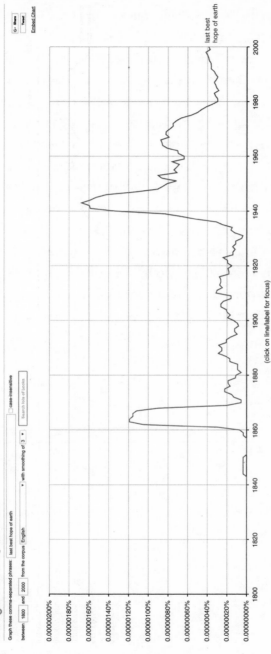

Figure 3. A comparison using Ngram Viewer of the relative usage frequency of two of Abraham Lincoln's phrases, 'better angels of our nature' and 'last best hope of earth'.

Google's Ngram Viewer allows searches for phrases of up to five words, displaying in return a graph of popularity in a corpus of books over a selected range of years (see Figure 3). The reader can then drill down into the actual examples, and assess the value of the return. (Most obviously, it is possible to clarify whether the system has identified a quoted extract, or simply a printing of the original source—for example, a nineteenth-century edition of Shakespeare's plays rather than a quotation from Shakespeare in the work of a later author.) We are constantly assailed by real and apocryphal quotations from a bewildering variety of spoken, written, and online sources. The world of quotations is constantly expanding, and infinitely diverse, and appearances of authority should often be treated sceptically. Nevertheless, for those interested in quotations, there has never been a better time to explore the phenomenon for themselves.

CHAPTER 1

BUT WHERE DO YOU FIND THEM?

A ny editor of a dictionary of quotations is likely to have encountered the question *But where (or how) do you find them?* A more pertinent question, however, also relating to the putative reader, might be *Why do you look for them?*—what is the primary purpose for which a dictionary of quotations has been compiled? Today, where the editor is concerned, there are likely to be two key reasons. First, to provide a resource that will answer the question *Who said that?* (sometimes with the subsidiary question *What was the exact wording of what was written or said?*). Secondarily, the collection may be aimed at satisfying the needs of readers who want a telling quotation to enhance their own speech or writings (often today, of course, including personal websites and social media).

We all have a personal vocabulary of remembered or half-remembered sayings, from sources ranging from Shakespeare and the Bible to advertising slogans. (In earlier centuries, the practice of 'learning by heart' meant that a whole range of poetic material was likely to be available to the memory, even if imperfectly.) At some point there is likely to be a desire to verify what we recall. A leading article in the *Times Literary Supplement* of 23 October 1919 considered how quotations function in the language. The leader-writer distinguished two main traditions of quotation. The first,

representing an appeal to authority, was that of classical quotation, deriving chiefly from 'the reasonable veneration of antiquity
which informed the Revival of Learning', although also probably
reinforced by the tradition of the *sortes* (the *sortes*, or more fully
sortes biblicae, involved the chance selection of a passage from the
Bible or other authoritative text as a method of divination or the
seeking of guidance). The second (described as the 'modern, allusive way') was the process involved when a writer or speaker
reached for the words of another because they expressed precisely
what he or she wanted to say.

Wise Sayings

The earliest collections of quotations were compilations of wise
sayings rather than current utterances, and were put together for
personal use. Scholars would collect passages important for reference into 'commonplace books', a term currently dated by the
Oxford English Dictionary to the sixteenth century. Thomas Cooper
(c.1517–94), theologian and lexicographer, refers to the process in
the introduction of the 1578 edition of his *Thesaurus*, advising that
'a studious young man ... may gather to himselfe good furniture
both of words and approved phrases ... and to make his use as it
were a commonplace booke'.[1] The commonplace tradition was to
have a long history, and indeed has survived into modern times.
In the twentieth century, it was the origin of *A New Dictionary of
Quotations*, published in America in 1942, compiled by the literary
critic H. L. Mencken (1880–1956). As Mencken wrote in the preface, the book was based on a collection of quotations that he had
begun in 1918 for his own use. 'Its purpose was to keep track of

sayings that, for one reason or another, interested me and seemed worth remembering, but that, also for one reason or another, were not in the existing quotation-books.'[2]

Literary Models

At the beginning of the eighteenth century, the writer Edward Bysshe published his three-part *The Art of Poetry*. While the first two sections offered respectively rules for verse-making and a dictionary of rhymes, the third part was intended to provide linguistic models for aspiring writers. Entitled 'A collection of the most natural, agreeable, & noble thoughts … that are to be found in the best English poets', it has a claim, in its systematic organization of extracts from his chosen writers, to be the first dictionary of quotations as we would understand the term today.

Bysshe was apparently alive to the dangers of plagiarism, and therefore assigned attributions to his quotations:

> Being very unwilling it should ever be laid to my charge, that I had furnish'd tools, and given a temptation of versifying, to the debasers of rhyme, and dabblers in poetry, I resolv'd to place these, the principal materials, under the awful guard of the immortal Milton, Dryden, &c.[3]

It is not clear whether he considered the possibility that his readers would simply use the book as a source for attributed (or unattributed!) quotations for direct employment in their own texts rather than offering models to be imitated.[4] Of course, Bysshe was providing examples of poetry, so the impact on prose may not have been at the forefront of his mind. Whatever the purpose, the

principle of identifying the author of a selected passage was established. It can be informative, however, to look in more detail at some
of the writers and passages that Bysshe considered as suitable as
impressive models, and consider to what degree we might expect
to find those passages surviving in a dictionary of quotations today.

Bysshe's collection is subject-organized, with his chosen passages grouped under themes. 'Ambition' is an early heading, and it
is not surprising to find the line warning against 'vaulting ambition that o'erleaps itself' from Shakespeare's *Macbeth*. The expression is certainly part of the public vocabulary today. It turned up,
for instance, in a column in the *Toronto Sun* of November 2016, in a
reflection on the defeated candidate in the US presidential election:

> When you lose an election to someone looked upon as a buffoon,
> only vaulting ambition of Macbethian proportions ... would obscure
> the graph showing your popularity was already worse than any
> established politician ever to seek the presidency of the United
> States.[5]

On the other hand, the following lines are not likely to strike much
of a chord today:

> Ambition is the dropsy of the soul,
> Whose thirst we must not yield to, but controul.

They come from the play *Antony and Cleopatra* (1677), by the writer
and politician Charles Sedley (bap. 1639–1701). The *Oxford Dictionary
of National Biography* calls Sedley 'a gifted dramatist, but not of the
first rank', and it seems unlikely that these lines ever had great
popular familiarity. (Dryden's *All for Love*, another reworking
of Shakespeare's play, first performed in 1678, was much more

successful.) Similarly, under 'Chaos', current dictionaries of quotations are likely to include these words from the second book of Milton's *Paradise Lost* (1667):

> Chaos umpire sits
> And by decision more embroils the fray.

However, it is much less likely that modern collections will have another of Bysshe's selections—'Here his forsaken seat old Chaos keeps' from *The Dispensary* (1699) by the English poet and physician Samuel Garth.

Changing Choices

It is instructive to compare Bysshe's choice with what we might expect to find in a dictionary of quotations today. Some of the authors chosen—for example, Thomas Otway and John Suckling—may hardly be represented, but Dryden, Shakespeare, and Pope are still widely quoted today. It is, however, possible to skim through many pages of Bysshe's chosen extracts before hitting on a quotation that would now be regarded as 'familiar', such as 'a little learning is a dangerous thing' (Pope), or 'great wits are sure to madness near allied' (Dryden). As well as this, a number of what we would consider famous quotations today appear in a variant form. To take one example, the Shakespeare section in The *Oxford Dictionary of Quotations* predictably includes Enobarbus' description of Cleopatra, when

> The barge she sat in, like a burnished throne,
> Burned on the water.

The entry includes a cross reference to lines from T. S. Eliot's *The Waste Land*:

> The Chair she sat in, like a burnished throne,
> Glowed on the marble.

As well as Eliot's allusive reference, evidence for continuing use within the language (on which inclusion in the *Oxford Dictionary of Quotations* rests) can be shown to stretch from Samuel Johnson's *Dictionary*, in which it was used to illustrate the entry for 'barge', to a twenty-first-century example in the *Daily Mail* of 15 June 2013. A columnist writing about the 1950s socialite Lady Docker commented: 'Her only function now was to be motored hither and thither to parties, sitting on her burnished throne like Cleopatra.' However, if we go back to Edward Bysshe's *The Art of English Poetry* (1702), we find something surprising. Cleopatra does indeed appear, but not as we might expect. Under the section 'Beauty', instead of quoting Shakespeare, Bysshe chooses the matching passage from Dryden's *All for Love*, beginning 'Her Gally down the Silver *Cydnus* row'd', and with no mention of a burnished throne (see Figure 4). From Bysshe's perspective, Dryden's version presumably offered a more classical and appropriate model for aspiring writers. In other places, Shakespeare is quoted directly, but sometimes the text has been modified. Macbeth's 'Tomorrow, and tomorrow, and tomorrow' speech is quoted in full, but instead of the lines

> Tomorrow, and tomorrow, and tomorrow,
> Creeps in this petty pace from day to day
> To the last syllable of recorded time;
> And all our yesterdays have lighted fools
> The way to dusty death

(23)

Beauty, thou art a fair but fading Flow'r,
The tender Prey of ev'ry coming hour:
In Youth, thou, Comet-like, art gaz'd upon,
But art portentous to thy self alone:
Unpunish'd, thou to few wert ever given,
Nor art a Blessing, but a Mark from Heaven. *Dryd.*
Merab the first, *Michal* the younger nam'd:
Both equally for diff'rent Glories fam'd:
Merab with spacious Beauty fill'd the sight;
But too much Awe chastis'd the bold delight:
Like a calm Sea, which to th' enlarged View,
Gives Pleasure, but gives Fear and Rev'rence too:
Michal's sweet looks clear and free Joys did move,
And no less strong, tho' much more gentle Love:
Like Virtuous Kings, whom men rejoice t' obey;
Tyrants themselves less absolute than they.
Merab appear'd like some fair Princely Tow'r:
Michal, some Virgin Queen's Delicious Bow'r.
All Beauties strove in little and in great,
But the contracted Brows shot fiercest heat.
From *Merab's* Eyes, fierce and quick Lightnings came;
From *Michal's*, the Sun's mild, yet active Flame.
Merab, with comely Majesty and State,
Bore high th' advantage of her worth and Fate.
Such humble Sweetness did soft *Michal* shew,
That none who reach so high, e'er stoop so low;
Merab rejoic'd in her rack'd Lover's Pain;
And fortify'd her Virtue with Disdain:
The Grief she gave, gave gentle *Michal* Grief;
She wish'd her Beauties less for their Relief. *Cowl.*

CLEOPATRA in her *GALLY.*

Her Gally down the Silver *Cydnos* row'd,
The Tackling Silk, the Streamers wav'd with Gold:
The gentle Winds were lodg'd in Purple Sails:
Her Nymphs, like *Nereids* round her Couch were plac'd,
Where she, another Sea-born *Venus*, lay.
She lay, and lean'd her Cheek upon her Hand,
And cast a look so languishingly sweet,
As if secure of all Beholders Hearts,
Neglecting she could take 'em. Boys, like *Cupids*,
Stood fanning with their painted Wings, the Winds

B 4 That

Figure 4. A page from Edward Bysshe's compilation of quotations
The Art of English Poetry, showing his preference for Dryden over
Shakespeare in the lines depicting Cleopatra in her 'Gally'.

We have:

> Tomorrow, tomorrow, and tomorrow
> Creep in a stealing pace from day to day
> To the last minute of revolving time;
> And all our yesterdays have lighted fools
> To their eternal homes.

There does not, however, appear to be any usage evidence to suggest that the last two lines did anything to replace 'the way to dusty death' as a Shakespearean quotation in the language.

Usage Guidance

Bysshe's professed intention was to provide quotations as rhetorical models to be items to be imitated rather than borrowed—an approach that could be seen as offering some level of usage guidance. This concept was developed much more strongly at the end of the eighteenth century by a publication that centred on the compilation of classical tags with some modern foreign-language words and phrases. This was the highly popular *A Dictionary of Quotations* by D. E. Macdonnel, first published in 1797 and forming the basis of later collections.[6] Its core material, as described in the introduction to the sixth edition of 1811, consisted of 'classic flowers, culled and retained from the poets of the Augustan age, or of apophthegms, and technical phrases, the pith and point of which are not easily transferred into another language'. While the primary purpose of this collection was to decode, advice was also provided as to when a particular expression could most appropriately be used. The entry for Horace's

Dulce et decorum est pro patria mori provided the translation 'It is pleasing and honourable to die for one's country'. It also added a warning about over-use: 'This is an apothegm cited in all wars, and in all ages. But sound philosophy will confine its application to the single case of our country's being attacked.'

Familiar Quotations

Bysshe and Macdonnel both offered guidance on how extracts from admired authors might be imitated or used. However, in the nineteenth century, there was an increasing focus on the concept of readers' need to remind or discover for themselves the precise wording or source of a quotation—either because it had been encountered in the work of another, or because their own remembrance of the details was imperfect.

In his 2003 exploration of the origins of John Bartlett's *Familiar Quotations*, Michael Hancher considers the origin of the expression 'household words', tracing it back to Shakespeare.[7] He further demonstrates that while the phrase 'familiar quotations' has now become almost synonymous with 'Bartlett's', the expression had already been used in other titles.[8]

A compilation of 'familiar' quotations is primarily one to which readers would turn to identify (or remind themselves of) the precise wording of a quotation, or details of its source. However, even at an early period Bartlett's collection could be used for another purpose. Michael Hancher quotes Bartlett's brother-in-law Joseph Willard as commenting that to 'the frequenters of his bookstore' he was 'an authority' who was able to provide them with 'the sources of apt or quotable phrases'.[9] As Hancher rightly points out:

Willard's equivocal phrase, 'the *sources* of *apt* or *quotable* phrases' (emphasis added), captures a double function for Bartlett's book. For more than a century, many users have gone to an edition of Bartlett's Familiar Quotations to find phrases to quote in their speeches or writing—that is, to find 'quotable phrases'.[10]

He goes on to say that this function 'is commonly ignored in Bartlett's prefaces', and it is probably fair to add that in this regard Bartlett is hardly singular. However, the ruthless employment by readers of collections of quotations to ornament their own work was a well-established custom even in Bartlett's day. And by the end of the nineteenth century there were significant compilations addressed to this need.

Quotable Sayings

The capacity of a dictionary of quotations to provide material that could be used to impress others is something that was explicitly noticed in the nineteenth century. An advertisement for a later edition of Macdonnel's dictionary, which appeared in 1833, reproduced a sentence from the *Literary Gazette*: 'A very ample and well-constructed Dictionary, by the aid of which any man may appear to be a learned clerk and deep scholar with wonderfully small trouble.' This aim seems to have been the genesis of a compilation made by the writer and translator Henry George Bohn.[11] In July 1867 he put out a private printing of what in 1881 was published as *A Dictionary of Quotations*. In the 1881 introduction, Bohn explained the genesis of the book. He had begun a private collection of quotations because he belonged in his youth to a group of 'exuberant youths' who competed with each other in 'spicing their conversation with scraps of poetry, sometimes Latin, but oftener English'. The collection of quotations had been a key tool by which he was able to impress his friends, although in fairness to Bohn it must be pointed out that he did compile the collection himself, rather than simply making use of the efforts of another.

Across the Atlantic, in 1882, the appearance of the *Cyclopædia of Practical Quotations*, edited by Jehiel Keeler Hoyt and Anna L. Ward, saw the arrival of a substantial compilation apparently with the stated purpose of providing 'a practical addition in composition'. While one function of the book might be to provide a source for a particular quotation, 'those who need merely suggestive thoughts will readily find what they wish under one of the numerous heads'. The 'Guide to the Use of the Book' for a revised edition of 1896 spelled out explicitly the dual principal functions: 'In consulting the volume it is supposed that each reader has one of two objects: either to find a quotation applicable to some topic under consideration, or to find one of which he has not a clear remembrance and of which he desires to know the exact reading.'

Just over ten years later, William Gurney Benham's *Cassell's Book of Quotations*, published in Britain in 1907, had a similar statement of intent. As the preface stated: 'This book is a collection of what is quotable as well as what is quoted.' Some items had found their place through usage evidence, but others (presumably the 'quotable' sayings) 'have seemed likely to be of general acceptability and usefulness, as "words which come home to men's business and bosoms"'.[12]

A reviewer in *T. P.'s Weekly* for that year reflected that the publication could be seen as 'a boon and a blessing' to 'the journalist and the speech maker', as well perhaps to a clergyman composing a sermon. In particular, a journalist composing an obituary notice might be found 'eagerly culling these useful quotations' for appropriate words. In sum, then, the purpose of compilation had shifted over time from the provision of rhetorical models, through the development of a work of reference to establish sources, to the practical purpose of supplying pithy expressions to be quoted by others.

Fleeting Fame

One of the most challenging parts of an editor's work can be assessing which recent utterances should go into a dictionary. High-profile items may be just those about which the reader has a question: Who said it first? What *exactly* was the wording, and on what occasion was it said? On the other hand, to what degree can we assume that something that catches the public attention at a particular moment has any real longevity? In 1963, Mandy Rice-Davies's riposte 'He would, wouldn't he?' might well not have been a pick for long-term survival. Conversely, an obituary of 2003 flagged up a largely forgotten instance from the same period where a contemporary prediction for lasting general fame was clearly wrong.

In February 2003, the *Daily Telegraph* carried an obituary for a former judge, Lord Wilberforce (1907–2003). Reviewing his judicial career, the obituary referred to a case, heard in 1964, in which relatives of a testator had challenged a bequest to the Francis Bacon Society to fund a search for documents that would prove Bacon's authorship of Shakespeare's plays. The judge ruled that the bequest was valid, even if the search were regarded as a wild-goose chase. 'Wild geese can, with good fortune, be apprehended.'

According to *The Times*, he had 'pronounced a dictum that will surely survive the sayings of the week and go into the dictionaries of quotations'.[13] However, in the twenty-first century the only references to Lord Wilberforce's dictum I have found come in his obituary, and a later obituary for one of the barristers involved in the case.[14]

What Do Readers Really Want?

In the twenty-first century, prospective dictionary-users can have recourse to print collections organized by author (to answer the question 'Who said that?') and by subject (to answer the question 'What's been said about this?'). There are also significant collections that have focused on providing a usage history for quotations that today are typically quoted in an altered form. Nigel Rees's *Cassell Companion to Quotations*, to take one example, was compiled for the stated purpose of providing 'context for, and ancillary information about', quotations that are part of the general vocabulary, attested by usage evidence.[15] The result is a fascinating and erudite collection, but the extra content and therefore extent needed for each entry necessarily restrict the overall number of quotations that can be covered in a print publication. Fred Shapiro's 2006 *Yale Book of Quotations*, while being a much more substantial volume, has to some degree been similarly impacted. The virtue of the approach is clear when looking, for example, at the entry in the *Yale Book* for Sam Goldwyn: the reader is not merely told which attributed quotations are likely to be apocryphal, but also given details of the sources by which they reached the general public. On the other hand, large-scale (in the range of

20,000 quotations) collections, such as the *Oxford Dictionary of Quotations* and *Bartlett*, try to serve the needs of the reader who wants both to look up an item about which there is no dispute, and to clarify the status of those more difficult items that are frequently misquoted and misattributed. This may mean that a more truncated treatment of problematic entries is required to permit inclusion of less-disputed items.

Sayings of the Week

Not every collection of quotations for general use was compiled in book form. Since the nineteenth century, newspapers and journals have brought together clusters of topical or otherwise related quotations for the enjoyment of their readers, as the development of the expression 'sayings of the week' to signal a cluster of recent high-profile utterances attests. Tracing it back, although there are one or two nineteenth-century 'outliers' (such as a column headed 'Some wise sayings of the week' in *Funny Folks*, 27 October 1883), the crystallization of the heading as something that was to become familiar seems to have come at the beginning of the twentieth century, when the *Observer* began to include a column of current utterances deemed to have caught the attention of the public, under the heading 'Sayings of the Week'.[16] The first instance I have found appeared on 18 March 1906, and the first saying given was 'enough of this foolery', attributed to the then prime minister, Sir Henry Campbell-Bannerman—an instance whose history bears further examination.

The expression was clearly not a new one in 1906. It can, for example, be found in the mid-nineteenth century, in *The Ways of the Hour* (1850) by the American novelist J. Fenimore Cooper.[17] But the words were used in the House of Commons by Campbell-Bannerman on an occasion that garnered attention. The occasion was a debate on free trade held in the House of Commons on 12 March 1906. The Liberals had been returned to government on a landslide in January, and the new prime minister, Campbell-Bannerman, was responding to questions put by the former prime minister, and new leader of the opposition, Arthur Balfour. He wound up, crushingly, by saying that he had no direct answer to give to them.

> They are utterly futile, nonsensical, and misleading. They were invented by the right hon. Gentleman for the purpose of occupying time in this debate. I say, enough of this foolery! It might have answered very well in the last Parliament, but it is altogether out of place in this Parliament. The tone and temper of this Parliament will not permit it. Move your Amendments, and let us, get to business.[18]

At this period, the London *Times* regularly carried reports of parliamentary debates, and the *Times* coverage for 12 March 1906 includes a version of Campbell-Bannerman's words, and assertion that he had no answer to give to Balfour's questions, which were 'futile, nonsensical, and misleading. They were invented to occupy time, and he said "Enough of this foolery." (Loud cheers.).'[19] Perhaps most tellingly, it was quoted back critically to the Liberal government by the Conservative Andrew Bonar Law in 1909. '"Enough of this foolery," we were told. "Free Trade is Free Trade, and that is an end of it."'[20]

'Enough of this foolery' then appeared five days later in the *Observer*, and there is also evidence that it gained some currency in political circles, at least during that parliament. It turns up in

May 1906, in a Lords debate, when Lord Newton used them to express a particular scepticism, saying that, if he were inclined to imitate what he called 'the somewhat uncourtly language of the present Prime Minister', he would be 'inclined to exclaim, with regard to all these Committees and Commissions, "Enough of this foolery"'.[21] In the following year, Lord Castlereagh referred to 'the now historic words of the Prime Minister, "Enough of this foolery"'.[22]

Campbell-Bannerman's is no longer a name to conjure with, and it is not surprising that we do not find contemporary references of this kind. What is interesting, however, is that in a historical context they do have some longevity. The *Oxford Dictionary of National Biography* entry for Campbell-Bannerman, describing his prowess as a parliamentary performer, speaks of his 'assured and effective performances from the dispatch box—most notably his verbal lashing of Balfour's dialectical meanderings as "foolery"'.[23] And, in 2008, the journalist Justin Webb used 'Enough of this foolery' as the heading for a blog. In the text, he compared the then presidential candidate Barack Obama with Campbell-Bannerman, evoking the occasion in 1906 when Campbell-Bannerman crushed the aggressive speech of the Leader of the Opposition. Quoting at some length from the speech, he concluded: 'This is the crux of the Obama case—"enough of this foolery". If America buys it, McCain is sunk.'[24] (I find it of real interest to hear that Webb says that the speech was one that he 'read as a schoolboy', and that still gives him pleasure today—another instance of the way in which a personal vocabulary of quotations can ensure that a particular item is passed on.)

From 1906, the *Observer* column became a settled item. The poet and literary editor John Collings Squire (1884–1958) wrote in 1921 that 'nothing in the *Observer* pleases me more that than little cage of "Sayings of the Week" in which the best things of our wits rub shoulders with the most alarming predictions of our geologists and eugenists'.[25] By 1932 the concept was so well established that the *Week-End Review* was able to use it as the basis of a competition:

> We offer a First Prize of One Guinea and a Second Prize of Half-a-Guinea for a set of six Sayings of the Week which, suitable for quotation in the Sunday papers, might have emanated respectively from those distinguished soothsayers: Mr Justice McCardie, Mr Robert Lynd, the President of the Royal Academy, Judge Cluer, Mr Hugh Walpole, and Bishop Welldon.[26]

'Sayings of the week' in effect represented a first attempt to bring together quotations of the moment. They needed to be reasonably pithy, and there was an assumption that they would emanate from someone with a reasonably high public profile. It was not required that they should have lasting qualities, although there was always the possibility that one or more of them might demonstrate longevity. But, essentially, they were a gathering for that particular week, and their selection would have required elements of the approach of someone editing a much larger and more permanent collection.

Looking to the Future

Collections of current utterances offered by periodicals provided a first taste of ways in which readers could access potentially popular material that had not necessarily been subjected to significant editorial scrutiny or verification. The next stage, of course, has been the provision of online resources—not so much the broader resources of the Internet as a whole (although that is a factor), but sites that are dedicated to quotations. The *Quote Investigator* site (http://quoteinvestigator.com/) (see Figure 5) focuses on tracing the origins of quotations whose attribution is disputed or unknown, and has the great advantage that questions about new items can be registered, and comments and new information from contributors can be added. Restrictions of space are not an issue.

Sites like *Brainy Quote* (www.brainyquote.com) offer a wide variety of material, including quotations on given topics, motivational

First They Ignore You, Then They Laugh at You, Then They Attack You, Then You Win

Mohandas Gandhi? Jean Cocteau? Robbie Williams? Julian Beck? Earl B. Morgan? Tony Benn? Peter D. Jones? Louis Agassiz? Arthur Schopenhauer?

Dear Quote Investigator: Mahatma Gandhi famously employed nonviolent strategies during the struggle for Indian independence. A quotation often attributed to him asserts that popular movements pass through four stages:

First they ignore you. Then they laugh at you. Then they attack you. Then you win.

I have been unable to find a good citation. Are these really the words of Gandhi?

Quote Investigator: Several researchers have attempted to find these words in Gandhi's oeuvre without success. The saying was ascribed to him by 1982, but Gandhi died decades earlier in 1948.

Figure 5. *Quote Investigator's* page for a supposed Gandhi quotation.

and inspirational quotations, and extra information about significant anniversaries or particular authors. Such sites could prove a rich resource for anyone wanting a telling phrase for a speech or presentation, or even for more personal use. The danger, or course, is that the attribution given may not be a solid one. Nevertheless, separately and together such sites offer a significant resource, and one to which more conventional collections need to respond. Perhaps in the end it does come down to the question of balance: bringing together in one place a coherent collection of material that readers are likely to want, and on whose provision they can rely.

Intelligent Elasticity And Comparative Levity

Whether a compilation is made in manuscript or print form or online, the challenges for an editor are likely to be the same. Ultimately, it comes down to editorial judgement based on the central character of your collection, and your understanding of what your readers want and expect. The archives of the Oxford University Press illuminate the process through some specific examples of editorial considerations and decisions during the compilation of the first three editions of *The Oxford Dictionary of Quotations*.

In June 1915, R. M. Leonard, one of the editors employed in Oxford University Press's London business, wrote to the London manager Humphrey Milford with a proposal (see Figure 6).[27] 'What do you think of an Oxford Dictionary of Poetry Quotations (not foreign quotations) based on Oxford texts and the N.E.D.?' He suggested as a model a collection that he described as 'a Yankee

TELEGRAMS:
  LENLEAGER. CANNON. LONDON.
TELEPHONE: CITY 4138.

9, Queen Street Place,
London, E.C.
June 23rd 1915

Dear Mr. Milford,

What do you think of an Oxford Dictionary of Poetry
Quotations (not foreign quotations), "based on Oxford texts
and the N E.D.?"

It could not be ready for 18 months.

My idea would be to give the quotations under subjects,
i.e., under Fame on p. 1225

Fame is the spur, etc.

K.   Milton Lycidas l. 70, [which would be indexed
F. is the spur K. 125.

There would be some classes within classes, i.e.,
month$

There would be a topical index, a list of authors with
births and deaths, but no reference to quotations as they would
be too numerous, Shakespeare's, for instance.

I have in mind Hoyt & Ward's Dictionary (5th edition
1883), a Yankee production six times as useful as any of the
English books arranged under the authors' names, and I have used
it for 20 years regularly. H. & W.'s printed page measures
$4\frac{1}{4}$ X 7, and their English quotations, poetry and prose, fill
500 double column pages, the index of authors, 10 pp., the

Figure 6. Letter from R. M. Leonard to Humphrey Milford, 23 June 1915,
proposing the compilation of an 'Oxford Dictionary of Poetry
Quotations'.

Dictionary of Poetical Quotations.

Allibone.   Chaucer to Tennyson. Quotations are here indexed
to authors, i.e., Shakespeare 40 lines X 10 - 400 references.

Pages 788.

Authors 550

Subjects 435

Quotations 13600

Dictionary of Prose Quotations.

Lippincott. 1886. Quotations also indexed as above.

Pages 764

Authors 544

Subjects 571

Quotations 8810

Size of page - 7 X 4½ - double columns.

In neither case are there references in text.

Lippincott 1881.

Figure 6. *Continued*

topical index (3 columns) 4 pp., and the index to first lines,
220 pp., but this is unnecessarily big, especially as the book
cost, I think, nearly 20/-.

Yours very truly
R. M. Leonard

Figure 6. *Continued*

production six times as useful as any of the English books arranged under authors' names'.[28] He provided further details as to its excellences, and must have provided a copy, since the following month Milford returned it. 'The index in this loathly Hoyt—returned herewith with thanks—is of course absolutely useless, not being alphabetical.'[29] Milford was, despite this, interested enough to ask if Leonard could provide a 'shortish' specimen, but if he did it has not come down to us. It is not until 1931 that we find the project being actively pursued, in a letter from the then Secretary to the Delegates (the Press's senior executive officer), R. W. Chapman, probably to the Assistant Secretary Kenneth Sisam.[30] In this letter, he gives a picture of what they would want their collection to contain, and it is clear that they had already extended the original suggestion of 1915:

> What one wants is to look for things off the beaten track of Bartlett etc., particularly (1) the really familiar things in other languages like Non tali auxilio [a tag from the *Aeneid* which in full means 'Neither the hour requires such help, nor those defenders'], (2) modern quotations that have not yet got into the books.[31]

The next stage was for Sisam to request a memorandum on the qualities and defects of the current Bartlett, and indeed on any other current collections. He raised the question of how to deal with major sources such as Shakespeare and the Bible. Chapman thought that to keep matters under control it would be necessary to limit themselves to what was 'eminently *quotable* and constantly quoted', rather than what was familiar. The Classics were also a consideration: if the book were not to be limited to English, it would seem illiterate to give 'a mere handful of classical tags'. There were grounds for a more generous selection: English authors habitually used 'a great many classical quotations; which most people can't find by going to Lewis & Short or the like'. It would, however, be essential to give translations. The upshot of this was that another of the London editors, Frederick Page, was set to produce an account of the competition.

The memorandum combines description and recommendation.[32] Page came down strongly on the side of a subject-organized text, provided, as he said, that the subjects were what he called 'real subjects'. At least three of the collections he examined seemed to him to fail on this count. His assessment is worth quoting, because it reflects both an appropriate description between a subject and a keyword, and an unconscious assumption that the editor's world view is to be shared by any prospective reader:

> They have subjects such as 'Presbyterians', 'Sheep', 'Shepherds', and these are not real subjects, though of course they are keywords. 'Presbyterian' is not a real subject, because the normal man can get through a long life respectably without ever having to think about Presbyterianism connotatively, but he cannot get through it without having to think about Puritanism and Clericalism as tendencies.[33]

As a result, quotations such as 'New Presbyter is but old Priest writ large' (Milton), ''Twas Presbyterian true blue' (Samuel Butler, *Hudibras*), and 'There was a Presbyterian cat' (from an anonymous song) would appear under headings like 'Priests, or Clergy, or Puritanism, or Sectarianism, anyhow something very general'.

The memorandum was considered by Chapman and Sisam. Chapman, describing himself as 'an impenitent authorian', was not persuaded by the concept of subject organization. He annotated the memorandum: 'Very ingenious; but nine times out of ten I should not think of what subject heading to turn to. I think it too difficult for human power.'[34] Sisam, on the other hand, saw difficulties with ordering by author.[35] How, for instance, were anonyma to be dealt with? And, in any case, if he knew an author, he could look up a concordance—a comment presumably indicating the expectation that quotations would be taken from authors regarded as significant enough for a concordance to their works to exist. However, tellingly, he was unable to propose a solution to the overall question of arrangement. He wanted good indexes of subjects, authors, and keywords, to a quotations text in alphabetical order, 'arranged on some practical principle'.

From the perspective of the twenty-first century, it may be thought that what Sisam wanted was the accessibility of an online text (see Figure 7). The sequential ordering was less important to him than the ability to approach individual items from a number of starting points. But, in 1931, the only choice was to decide on a formula that would work for hard copy, and Chapman's views carried the day. Sisam himself was aware of the need to arrive at a pragmatic solution. At the conclusion of his letter to Milford he added a cautionary publisher's comment:

> Obviously this work is not going to succeed if it takes up too much time, or if it becomes too bulky. There is money in it only on condition that we keep the scope and plan within easily manageable limits. My fear would be that it became too learned and recondite, whereas what we want is a book popular and useful, though accurate within its limits. And for that reason I am in favour of fixing on a plan— open to every kind of intelligent elasticity—at the outset, so that the field is limited and the number of harassing doubts reduced by a kind of 'code'.[36]

The book was to be author-organized, but what was to be in it? It is appropriate here to look back to the beginning of this section,

Oxford Dictionary of Quotations (8 ed.)

Edited by Elizabeth Knowles

Previous Edition (7 ed.)

'A glorious treasure-house for browsers' – *Times Literary Supplement*

Over 20,000 quotations

A major new edition of the most authoritative dictionary of quotations available brings you the wit and wisdom of past and present – from the ancients of East and West to the global village of the 21st century. Find that half-remembered line in a paradise of quotations for all occasions, from over 3,700 authors. Lord Byron may have taken the view: 'I think it great affectation not to quote oneself', but for the less self-centred this classic work provides a quote for every occasion, whether from the gr ... More

BIBLIOGRAPHIC INFORMATION

Publisher: Oxford University Press
Print ISBN-13: 9780199668700
Current Online Version: 2014
eISBN: 9780191758034

Print Publication Date: 2014
Published online: 2014
DOI: 10.1093/acref/9780199668700.001.0001

Elizabeth Knowles, *editor*

Elizabeth Knowles is a historical lexicographer who worked on the 4th edition of the *Shorter Oxford English Dictionary* (1993) and was Editor of the 5th, 6th, and 7th editions of the *Oxford Dictionary of Quotations* (1999, 2004, 2009). Her other editorial credits include the *Oxford Dictionary of Modern Quotations* (3rd edition, 2007), *What They Didn't Say: A Book of More*

Find at OUP.com

Figure 7. Screenshot showing the eighth edition (2014) of the *Oxford Dictionary of Quotations*, available electronically through *Oxford Reference Online* <www.oxfordreference.com>.

and the first letter from Leonard. His proposal was for a collection of poetry quotations: the material was to be from English literature and (primarily) standard authors—what we would now think of as the traditional canon.

By 1931 this had somewhat widened. Chapman was ready to include the 'really familiar' from other languages, and also, more daringly, modern quotations that did not yet appear in other collections. Sisam was still clear that 'non-English quotations must be reduced to very narrow limits' (partly, it must be said, on grounds of extent and cost). A distinction was to be drawn between what a French scholar would quote in French, and 'that rather small number of French phrases which are almost current English (or have been)'. Latin, he thought, would provide the bulk of the foreign quotations, with German, Italian, and Spanish being satisfied by a handful of tags. He was doubtful too about the degree to which classical Greek was now quoted, asking: 'Isn't it a fact that Greek has disappeared from the House of Commons?'

He went on to consider the collection of material, with the warning that 'even in English we shall have to guard against things quotable, as apart from things commonly quoted'. He thought from a practical point of view that it would be risky to have texts read by people who were devoted to them. 'They probably quote, or think they quote, those texts to an abnormal extent.' The result would be a flood of material, and preparatory work that was 'vast or uneven'.

In conclusion, then, they were looking at a dictionary of quotations that would have a primarily literary base, and that would include quotations from major writers likely to be quoted in English by the literate and cultured Englishman (or, indeed, Englishwoman).[37] The dictionary was finally published in 1941, and was warmly received. The *Illustrated London News* described it as having 'authority with charm', and by March 1942 Milford was reporting that the first printing of 20,000 was exhausted about a month after publication, and that for three months they had been struggling to get a reprint on to the market.[38] The selection had moved a considerable way since the initial proposal for a collection of poetry quotations. The selection was nevertheless pre-eminently a literary one, but popular material was represented, notably through advertising slogans. While undeniably Anglocentric, it represented a genuine attempt to satisfy the needs of a wide reading public.

The success of the dictionary meant that by 1949 a second edition was in hand. Geoffrey Cumberlege (since 1945 Publisher to Oxford University Press, in succession to Humphrey Milford) wrote to his predecessor that the time had come to start on a revision.[39] There was already 'an immense accumulation of suggestions' that would have to be sorted through by a committee, and F. W. Page had suggestions for what could be dropped: he had 'never much liked' such things as advertising slogans and lines from comic songs. Other possibilities for cutting were book titles and the opening lines of hymns, which he saw as tags rather than quotations—although, as he added, 'no one has successfully solved what is and is not a quotation'—a comment that goes to the heart of the editor's dilemma. Milford was enthusiastic, and clear in his views.

> What fun! F. P. would like to see all frivolities go—even 'Pop goes the weasel' and 'Daisy, Daisy'—but I vote emphatically for such genuinely popular quotations as those, while gladly getting rid of, e.g., 'Twiggez-vous', and advertising slogans (I can't cast my eyes on any at the moment).[40]

He added: 'I think the levity—comparative—of O.D.Q. is partly the reason for its success.'

A revision committee was set up, the first meeting of which was held at Amen House in London on 28 April 1949. They readopted the principles underlying selection for the first edition, and agreed to go through the text considering existing matter for deletion or rearrangement, as well as through suggestions for inclusion (it was agreed that any item receiving two votes should be included). Between 28 April 1949 and 10 August 1950 the committee met seventeen times, considering a wide range of material (the min-utes of the meeting on 5 May 1949 noted both Donne's prose and *The Wind in the Willows* as possible sources). More recent writers presented a particular challenge, as is evidenced by the case of the dramatist Christopher Fry (1907–2005). The year 1949 saw his successful *The Lady's Not for Burning*, and the question of how to treat this new writer was given anxious consideration. The min-utes of 8 September 1949 are worth quoting in detail, as they reveal some of the pressures, as well as the difficulty in coming to agreement. It was recorded that a number of suggestions from the play had been made, and that eight of them had been selected for inclusion.

> The question then arose whether their popularity was as yet estab-lished or whether they were only familiar to those who had seen the play, and whether they should wait for a new edition before being included. Mr. Toyne pointed out that one quotation from 'The Lady' had already been accepted, and as the new suggestions enjoyed as much popularity, these should logically be accepted as well. A sin-gle quotation only from this author would appear unrepresentative and out of place.[41]

It seems clear from what follows that this occasioned considerable, and possibly heated, discussion.

> Miss Hill thought that none should appear at all. Mr Goffin was in favour of including the one original suggestion on its own. Miss Pavey-Smith, Mr Ward and Mr Toyne seemed to favour the inclusion of all eight. It was eventually decided to submit the quotations in question to Mr Cumberlege and perhaps to Sir Humphrey Milford for verdict.

It appears that Cumberlege (and possibly Milford, if the question was put to him) agreed with Miss Hill in voting against the shock of the new: Fry did not appear until the third edition of 1979, when twenty-one quotations were included.[42] In fact, the difference in content between the first two editions was not great. The preface to the 1979 third edition summarized it as follows:

> The second edition, published in 1953, was about 95% the same in content as the first edition of 1941—the differences consisting then chiefly of the addition of Second World War quotations (essentially of course those of Winston Churchill), correction of errors, rearrangement of certain sections, and much more full and precise indexing.

Arrangements for the third edition began in 1970, and were heralded by a report from the writer and critic Marghanita Laski (1915–88), who since 1958 had been a voluntary reader contributing material to the files of the *OED Supplement*. She had been asked to make recommendations for an editorial policy, and the report included two suggestions that, if they had been adopted, would have changed the character of the dictionary forever. In the first instance, she suggested that quotations should be given in their original published form, rather than in the edited form of a standard reading edition. Noting that in any case Chaucer and Langland were appearing in Late Middle English, she gave the view (surely an optimistic one for the general reading public) that 'no subsequent original English text should present readers with any difficulty'.[43] Where possible, quotations should reflect the punctuation and spelling of the first edition. The spelling of many words would reflect not what the searcher would have encountered in their *Times* leader column, but (for example) the spelling of the King James Bible.

Her second suggestion, which would at least have reduced the number of difficult spellings from earlier centuries, related to content. She thought that the decade of the 1960s had seen what she called 'the vocabulary of classic quotation' being 'increasingly replaced with a body of popular quotation'. (By 'classic quotation', she explained, she meant 'quotation from English and other modern language literatures' and she gave the view that 'in this sense the use of classic quotation is now almost dead'.) In her experience: 'The references of leader writers nowadays are more likely to come from short-lived popular stock. Only old-fashioned people like myself still use classic quotations, and when we do, we are likely to be pulled up by our employers for being esoterically incomprehensible.' She went on: 'It seems a basic policy decision needs to be taken at the start; whether it is the function of the Dictionary to preserve the classic culture till it should be wanted again … or whether it is genuinely to represent the stock of quotable phrase in the modern more-or-less educated mind.'

Marghanita Laski was in no doubt as to the answer to the question posed. 'I am', she wrote, 'for the second alternative'. She did not, however, persuade the Press, as various comments in the file on her proposal over the following weeks show. Adverse opinions included the comment that the plan was 'far too radical for a proved best-seller' (2 July 1970); the hope that they 'would not yield to any temptation to produce a clever-dick collection' (3 July 1970); the view that the plan for revision as given would be not just wrong but 'in terms of publishing, probably suicidal' (19 August 1970); and the warning that the policy as suggested would not only 'destroy one of the best reference books' in the list, but be likely to 'replace it with a failure'.[44]

Rejection of the proposals was not based simply on conservatism. At the heart of the matter lay a clear view as to the function of the book: a work of popular reference that could be consulted about quotations encountered in a chronologically diverse range of sources. It was in that spirit that the committee of revisers set about their work, as before circulating new suggestions on prepared forms with a voting box for each item. (I have been told that three votes were necessary for inclusion.) 'Classic' material in the existing text was not viewed uncritically: according to the introduction, one of the revisers had commented on the necessity of clearing the 'huge snowdrifts of Wordsworth'. But the editors were determined on a book that served its readers by providing quotations from a mainstream and literary tradition. They were particularly concerned that the book should not be an 'anthology displaying the choice and taste of one man, or even of a small committee of the Press such as compiled the first edition of the *Dictionary*'. The challenge, as it still is today, was to anticipate what the reading public would be likely to look up.

CHAPTER 2

BORROWING WORDS

In the preceding chapter, I looked at the way in which dictionaries of quotations developed over the centuries, with particular consideration given to the work of compilers in response to the perceived needs of the market. In this chapter, I want to look at the dictionary-user, illuminating the picture with examples from fact and fiction. Individual works that were studded with quotations functioned effectively as the repository of extracts from respected sources, as demonstrated by Robert Burton's *Anatomy of Melancholy*. Burton, as J. B. Bamborough has said, deliberately brought together all that had been written on his chosen topic in 'a syncretic account of all the theories and observations on the subject of Melancholy'.[1] The result was a quotation-rich text that could be, and often was, plundered by others. This seems to have begun early. Anthony à Wood, having written of him in 1649 that 'no man in his time did surpass him for his ready and dextrous interlarding his common discourses among them with verses from the poets and sentences from classical authors', added that 'some authors have unmercifully stolen matter from the said book without any acknowledgement'.[2] Nearly a hundred years later, the antiquary and diarist Thomas Hearne (1678–1735) was to comment: 'No book sold better formerly than Burton's *Anatomy of Melancholy*, in which there is great variety of learning, so that it hath been a common-place for filchers.'[3] Burton's work was effectively an anthology of quotations.[4] Other writers, without quite such a wholesale approach, have used lines and sentences from the works of fellow authors to enhance their own texts, typically as epigraphs to title pages and as chapter headings.

Abominable Devices

William Makepeace Thackeray's mid-nineteenth-century novel *Pendennis* depicts an Irish journalist, Captain Shandon, who, in accordance with Hearne's comment on 'filchers', uses Burton's *Anatomy of Melancholy* as a key resource from which to adorn his writings: '"Hand me over the Burton's *Anatomy*, and leave me to my abominable devices," Shandon said, with perfect good-humour. He was writing, and not uncommonly took his Greek and Latin quotations (of which he knew the use as a public writer) from that wonderful repertory of learning.'[5]

Twenty years before, the eponymous hero of Edward Bulwer-Lytton's novel *Paul Clifford* (1830), acting as reviewer for a periodical entitled *The Asinaeum*, recalls 'the many extracts he had taken from *Gleanings of the Belles Lettres* in order to import elegance to his criticism'.[6] This dubious-sounding source presumably fulfilled for him much the same function as Burton's *Anatomy* did for the Captain. There were some dictionaries of quotations in Captain Shandon's day, but not the many solid volumes with which the twentieth century was to be provided. In April 1944, a *Times* leader on literary allusion, remembering the captain's technique, commented: 'Today the classics are out of fashion and the Captain's successors probably turn to *The Oxford Dictionary of Quotations*.' But the *ODQ* did not appear until 1941: before that, writers in search of telling phrases would have turned to other collections, not least Bartlett's *Familiar Quotations*.

Does Anyone Know Where?

Captain Shandon was frankly plundering someone else's text to augment his own, but other readers were more concerned to establish the source and precise form of a quote. The kind of process involved is illustrated in the British scholarly journal *Notes and Queries*, founded in 1849 with the explanatory subtitle '*a medium of inter-communication for literary men, artists, antiquaries, genealogists, etc.*'. The first page of the opening number carried an appropriate quotation from Dickens as a strapline: '"When found, make a note of it."—Captain Cuttle.' The final paragraph of the introductory article concluded: 'To our readers therefore who are seeking for Truth, we repeat "When found, make a Note of it;" and we must add, "till then make a Query".' In February 1850, a reader wrote to *Notes and Queries* to ask: 'Does anyone know where the oft-quoted line, "Praise undeserved is censure in disguise," is to be found? A long search for it has hitherto proved ineffectual.'[7] *Notes and Queries* was able to help. The response began: 'This line, which is so often quoted, with the variation "Praise undeserved is satire in disguise," is to be found in Pope's *First Epistle of the Second Book of Horace*.' However, its reader (evidently in common with others) had misquoted: the correct reading should have been: 'Praise undeserved is scandal in disguise.' The note went on to point out that in Warton's edition of Pope, as in A. Dyce's Aldine Poets edition, the line itself was marked as a quotation—could any of its correspondents trace the source from which Pope derived it? This was followed up on 9 February 1850 by a contribution from James H. Friswell, who confirmed that the correct quotation was: 'Praise undeserved is satire in disguise.'[8] It was 'by Mr Br—st, author of a copy of verses called the *British Beauties*'. He was unable to fill up the hiatus because he had no time to search the museum catalogue, although he thought it likely that 'the author belonged to the "mob of gentlemen who wrote with ease"'. Today one can imagine a similar question and answer taking place online—with the proviso that today we have a range of online texts to search for ourselves before reaching out more widely.

That Clever Little Thing I Heard Mr Williams Say

One example of possible use was postulated by Frederick Page when considering what might be desirable in a dictionary of quotations to be published by Oxford University Press. In the memorandum cited in the previous chapter, he adopted the persona of a prosaic-minded person, ignorant of Tennyson's poetry, who had to reply to the Commercial Travellers' toast at a staff dinner. 'I want to bring in that clever little thing I heard Mr Williams say once about "Quotations five words long".' He had supposedly heard Charles Williams (with whom in real life Page shared an office) quote Tennyson's lines:

> Jewels five-words-long
>   That on the stretch'd fore-finger of time
>   Sparkle forever.[9]

However, his unpoetic nature made it impossible for him to retain the jewel metaphor, and he would have been more likely to look for the passage under Shakespeare than Tennyson.

Page thought that the only hope for his would-be speaker would be a subject-organized book that had a section on quotations. He did not prevail in his recommendation, but he was probably right that his unpoetic speaker would not have run the words to earth in the ODQ. When it was published in 1941, the relevant quotation appeared under Tennyson, but to find it in the index would have required the searcher to have retained the keyword 'jewels'.

Learning and Latin

Reliance on classical sources has often occasioned comment, as two very different accounts show. In Raymond Surtees's novel *Handley Cross* (1854), a magazine editor attempts to acquire Mr Jorrocks as a hunting correspondent. A friend, writing on his behalf, explained that, if Jorrocks could supply accounts of runs, 'he would spice them up with learning and Latin. He has Moore's Dictionary of Quotations, and can come the classical quite as strong at the great Mr Pomponius Ego, whom they reckon the top-sawyer in that line.' In the twentieth century, Guy de la Bédoyère, a historian studying coins issued by the third-century Romano-British emperor Carausius, concluded that letter inscriptions on them, respectively R.S.R. and I.N.P.C.D.A., might refer to lines by Virgil. He decided to 'skim through Virgil', but initially decided that 'the easy thing to do would be to skim through the *Oxford Dictionary of Quotations*'. He turned to 'an old 1950s copy' and scanned through the Virgil entry, looking for lines that would offer the right initial letters.[10] He found what he was looking for: 'On page 557 column (a) I found I.N.P.C.D.A.' The relevant line (from the *Eclogues* of Virgil) was 'Iam nova progenies cœlo demittitur alto' ('Now a new and better race returns from on high'). He found R.S.R. in the second half of the preceding line, 'redeunt Saturnia regna' ('now Saturn is king again'). As he commented: 'I never even had to look up Virgil properly.' The story attests both to the practical value of a dictionary of quotations, and the editorial judgement, which included this passage of the *Eclogues* as something likely to be looked up.

Relying on the Dictionary

The idea of someone using a dictionary of quotations to put on a show of knowledge through apparent familiarity with the classics surfaces on a number of occasions. The London *Times* of 23 September 1908 carried a report of the International Press Congress held in Berlin. There was an address by the then German Chancellor, Bernhard, Prince von Bülow, in which he discussed his relations with the Press. His reputation, it appeared, was for heavy reliance on the standard German dictionary of quotations, Georg Büchmann's *Geflugelte Worte* ('Winged Words'), first published in 1864. As the *Times* account of his speech put it:

> He was convinced that there were really people who believed that he made his speech with a Büchmann dictionary of quotations by his side, a story circulated as a joke by a journalistic friend of his. In reality he always quoted from memory, but he was delighted to find caricatures of himself in the comic press with a Büchmann in his hand and a poodle by his side.

A news report of December 1905 had found it worth noting of a speech that 'Prince Bülow for once spoke without quotations', and

Bülow himself wrote later that, 'even when I was at school, I had a taste, or a weakness, for quotations'.[11] However, the assumption made by the cartoonists was inaccurate. As he averred: 'I never had a *Büchmann* in my hand until, after my resignation, his publisher sent me a beautifully bound copy with a friendly letter in which he said that the gift of the most famous of all his publications would have been misinterpreted while I was in office.' The publisher, presumably delighted by the free publicity received, now 'took the liberty' of sending what was presumably the latest edition, in which 'one or two utterances' of Bülow's had been tactfully included.

Bülow is far from being the only politician associated with the use of a dictionary of quotations, although he may well be one of the more famous. Over fifty years before his speech in Berlin, a Virginian called Edmund Ruffin recorded in his journal an account of a lately deceased local politician, William Stevenson. In his entry for 30 January 1857 Ruffin wrote of this 'corrupt and unprincipled politician':

> He was appointed a Visitor of the University, & Rector, or chairman of the board. He was little fitted by education for the government of an institute of learning. He had not even learned Latin, though he was in the habit & very fond of using commonplace Latin quotations in his speeches in Congress &c., which he obtained readily, with their meaning, from the 'Dictionary of Quotations'.[12]

Stevenson incurred Ruffin's scorn, but presumably avoided general public ridicule. This was not the case with an unfortunate Senator whose troubles were reported by the *Washington Post* of 12 February 1911. He became the victim of a con-trick, flattered by an invitation to contribute to what was claimed to be a de-luxe edition of 'Daily

Mottoes of our Modern Eminent and Self-made Men'. The purpose, of course, was to obtain specimens of this handwriting and stationery. As the *Washington Post* put it:

> Far into the night the Senator labored with the dictionary of quotations. He was not looking for a motto that he had ever lived or tried to live up to, but one that would get votes. On the theory that the less his constituency understood a motto the more they would think it contained a noble sentiment, he sent one that was a model of bombastic morality.[13]

His vanity resulted in his downfall, and the role of 'the dictionary of quotations' in allowing him to assume a fatal pretence of learning is clear.

As shown in the story of Edmund Ruffin and William Stevenson, the dictionary of quotations in question may not be specifically identified—it possibly exemplifies what the scholar of lexis and lexicography Rosamund Moon has called 'the UAD: the Unidentified Authorizing Dictionary, usually referred to as "the dictionary", but very occasionally as "my dictionary"'.[14] A modern example of this concept is provided by the introduction by Stephen Fry to Alastair Rolfe's compilation of Wilde sayings, *Nothing ... Except my Genius* (Penguin, 1997). In this case, the purpose is to find pithy sayings to enhance a person's own less striking prose. Discussing 'the point of Wilde', Fry considers why he was so much more than 'a possible source of inspiration when trawling the dictionary of quotations for a best man's speech'. The reference here, certainly, is to a generic compilation, not to any specific collection. This is the 'Unidentified Authorizing Dictionary' identified by Rosamund Moon, and the purpose for which it might be consulted is decidedly utilitarian.

In Alan Bennett's 2007 novel *The Uncommon Reader*, the Queen is talking to her amanuensis, Norman, and uses the words 'the road not travelled.' She adds:

> 'Who's that?'
> 'Who, ma'am?'
> 'The road not travelled. Look it up.'
> Norman looked it up in the *Dictionary of Quotations* to find that it was Robert Frost.[15]

It would be nice to think that this was the *Oxford Dictionary of Quotations* (capitalization and italicization might be taken to indicate an actual title), but that would pose the question of how Norman actually looked it up. 'The road not travelled' is actually an amalgam of the title of a poem (Robert Frost's 1916 'The Road Not Taken'), and the lines that run: 'Two roads diverged in a wood, and I— | I took the one less travelled by.'[16] The only index references at present are under 'roads' ('Two r. diverged') and 'travelled' ('the one less t.'). Bennett's version of the line offers a nice example of the difficulties that can be posed when trying to verify a misremembered reference. However, it does not invalidate the point that in the story this unidentified dictionary has functioned as an authority, in identifying the American poet Robert Frost as the author of the key words.

A Source of Authority

The *Oxford Dictionary of Quotations* is name-checked in one of John Mortimer's short stories about the barrister Horace Rumpole, in which (encouragingly for an editor) Rumpole is shown making careful and successful use of the keyword index to identify the author of two quotations. In 'Rumpole and the Official Secret', Rumpole is asked to defend a lady charged under the Official Secrets Act, who has supposedly revealed to the Press details of expenses at the Ministry of Defence in a letter beginning: 'Do you want to hear about tea and scandal, their ancient custom, in the Ministry of Defence?' The phrase 'tea and scandal' bothers Rumpole: 'Back in Froxbury Court I looked tea up in the Index of my old *Oxford Dictionary of Quotations*: "is there honey still for t.?" no, "sometimes counsel take—and sometimes t.", not that; and then I saw it: "t. and scandal".'[17]

Following the reference, he finds the full quotation: 'Retired to their tea and scandal, according to their ancient custom', from the dedication to Congreve's *Double Dealer*. He characterizes it as 'rather an obscure phrase' (a judgement that an NGram Viewer search supports, at least as far as the twentieth century is concerned), and subsequently this leads him to the detection of the real mole. In a conversation between the two men, the suspect refers to the aristocratic origins of the Permanent Under-Secretary of the department: 'Comes from "a branch of one of your ante-diluvian families, fellows that the flood couldn't wash away".' When Rumpole goes home, he once more consults his *Oxford Dictionary of Quotations*, and finds that this too is a quotation from Congreve (this time from *Love for Love*). Armed with this coincidence, he successfully tackles his suspect and secures the necessary admission.

Changing Editions?

A subset of the UAD referred to above might be the case in which a particular dictionary is identified, but where there is less awareness that the text might have changed throughout decades and editions. I have already described how a historian turning to the *ODQ* in 2012 reached naturally for his 'old 1950s copy'.[18] In 2004 I received a letter addressed to the Editor of the Oxford Dictionary of Quotations at Oxford University Press, Amen House, London (an address that the Press had left in 1966). Opening 'Gentlemen:', the letter expressed the correspondent's amazement that what he referred to as 'Robbie Burns' oft-quoted "The best-laid plans of mice and men"' did not appear to be included in the second edition of the *ODQ*. Our correspondent was writing from Canada, and he wondered whether the reason was that this was a familiar quotation only in America, where it had been popularized by the title of Steinbeck's novel *Of Mice and Men*.

This raised, of course, the immediate question of whether Burns's quotation was actually missed out of earlier versions—it was certainly in the sixth edition, published that autumn. When we looked, we ascertained that it had been in since the first edition of 1941. It seemed likely that our enquirer had been misled by his alteration of the line. Although 'the best-laid plans' is often misquoted today, the original text has 'the best-laid schemes'. It seems likely that he had looked up 'plans' in the keyword index and failed to find it. Beyond this, however, I was struck that there was no indication that he had looked to see whether a later edition might have rectified what he believed to be a fault.

Something similar might be suggested by a quotation used in the House of Lords in 1997. In response to Lord Henley's moving an Amendment, Lord Morris is reported as saying:

Accept a miracle instead of wit, See two dull lines with Stanhope's pencil writ.

I can see from the look on the face of the Minister that that is one quotation he does not recognise immediately, although a few moments with the *Oxford Dictionary of Quotations* will probably assist him. Those were the words of Edward Young in 1820 in Spence's Anecdotes.

It seems likely that the literary scholar Lord Morris (1930–2001) would have been acquainted with the writings both of the poet and dramatist Edward Young (1683–1785) and of the anecdotist Joseph Spence (1699–1768). He may, however, have been right in assuming that Lord Henley, at that point Minister of State for the Department of Education and Skills, had less familiarity to them. In his entry for Morris in the *Oxford Dictionary of National Biography*, the historian Keith Robbins has commented: 'His speeches, invariably laced with erudite quotation, could penetrate the rather less literary defences of government spokespersons.' Lord Henley, probably wisely, did not attempt to match him, but he did offer reassurance as to how well he was equipped. Admitting that the Young quotation would have been beyond him. He had brought 'a fairly large pile of documents' with him into the Chamber, but 'I think that to have brought with me the Oxford Dictionary of Quotations in anticipation of the wit of the noble Lord would not have been appropriate or necessary. No doubt those who advise me, if they have a moment, will look up these matters at some point.'

It would be interesting to know if any of his advisers did try to look up the Young quotation, and, if so, in which edition. Investigation of the *ODQ* reveals that such advice if given today would sadly be less than helpful. The first two editions (1941 and 1953) did include the quotation in the entry for Edward Young:

Accept a miracle, instead of wit,
See two dull lines, with Stanhope's pencil writ.
Written with Lord Chesterfield's Diamond Pencil.

Spence, *Anecdotes* (1820), p. 378

However, the quotation was dropped from the third edition of 1979, and it has never been reinserted. An online search of later sources supports the explanation that there was very little further evidence for the lines being quoted.

It seems likely to be the case that most people who acquire one of the main dictionaries of quotations are unlikely replace it with a later version. What is on their shelves becomes, for them, 'the' *Oxford Dictionary of Quotations*, or *Bartlett's Familiar Quotations*. It is worth at this point considering further the question of motive. As for Henry Bohn trying to impress his friends, the concern of the Senator criticized by the *Washington Post* was for personal status. However, professional writers may have very practical reasons for equipping themselves with quotable quotes.

Commercial Uses

In Dorothy L. Sayers's detective novel *Murder Must Advertise*, published in 1933, Lord Peter Wimsey takes on the persona of Mr Bredon, aspirant copywriter in an advertising agency. In the first chapter, Mr Bredon explores the office that has been assigned to him. As well as a dictionary and various other books, his bookcase contains '*Alice in Wonderland*, Bartlett's *Familiar Quotations*, the Globe edition of the *Works of Wm. Shakespeare*, and five odd numbers of the *Children's Encyclopedia*'. Bartlett is clearly a key source.

One strand of the plot concerns the need to provide headlines for 'Nutrax', a preparation designed to soothe troubled nerves. The copywriters accordingly seek out appropriate quotations. In chapter nineteen, we hear that the client firm has rejected a series of possible headlines, including 'If you have Tears' and 'O Say, What are you Weeping For?' Furthermore, the copywriter concerned had 'flown into a passion because the *Dictionary of Quotations* had mysteriously disappeared'. Sayers herself had been a successful copywriter in Benson's agency in the 1920s, and the convincing background of her story is held to have been based on her experiences there. It seems likely that the importance given to Bartlett as a key resource for the hard-pressed copywriter reflects reality.

Verifying your References

There are, of course, dangers in taking material directly from a dictionary of quotations—not least because you may be unaware of, or may misunderstand, the context from which the quotation has been taken. Of course, a number of quotations establish themselves so clearly in the public vocabulary that their original background is less important. However, there are risks, as the following story shows.

In 1974, following a British general election, the satirical journalist Bernard Levin published an article entitled 'Intimate Confessions of an Election Night Watcher'. In the course of it, he reflected on past and present political journalists as television presenters, with particular reference to David and Jonathan Dimbleby, sons of a famous father.

For the job of master of television ceremonies on election night there will never be anybody to touch Richard Dimbleby, a professionals' professional if ever there was one, and a man who illustrates to perfection the truth that heredity does not run in the family: the Dimbleboys are engaging fellows enough, but *stat magni nominis umbra*.[19]

A few days later, a response from one of the 'Dimbleboys', David Dimbleby, appeared in the Letters column. The first paragraph ran:

I used to attribute the profusion of Latin tags in Bernard Levin's prose either to his astonishing erudition or his powers of invention. Now I see I am wrong on both counts. His skill lies in scanning his book of quotations and selecting from it at random, regardless of context.[20]

He went on to point out that Lucan's line 'stat magni nominis umbra' ('he stands in the shadow of a great name') referred not to Pompey's sons standing in the shadow of their father's reputation, but to the ageing Pompey himself, overshadowed by the fame he himself had once had.

A dictionary of quotations can be seen as something of a Jekyll and Hyde. It may constitute an essential work of reference, offering us models of style and reminders of principle, as well as allowing us to trace an unknown or half-remembered quotation to its source. Less acceptably, however, it may tempt us into a pretence of scholarship, which we may inadvertently show to have been ill-founded, to our embarrassment. Unless, of course, we have the unashamed self-confidence of Surtees's editor planning to avail himself of Mr Jorrocks's services.

Nearer our own time, the literary scholar Marjorie Garber has called attention to a journalist's critique of a speech by the

Republican senator Henry Hyde at the hearings for the impeachment of President Clinton in January 1999.[21] The senator, as she pointed out, 'gave his remarks the requisite element of gravity by salting them with familiar quotations'. Analysing the speech, and commenting on its reception, Garber reports on two instances of journalistic coverage that related the significant use of quotations by Hyde to a well-known dictionary of quotations as the likely source. According to the *New York Times*, he had 'mustered a veritable Bartlett's in offering his last impassioned plea for conviction'. And a journalist for another newspaper had earlier summed up the speeches in the debate as 'blue suits quoting from Bartlett's'.[22] The implication of all these comments is that quotations were being taken from a useful source with the intention of adding significance to a speech, but without in fact doing more than rendering the argument slightly suspect for that reason.

A Place for Serendipity

It has, of course, to be admitted that on occasion recourse to a dictionary of quotations may be unavailing, as is evidenced by an account from the 1960s. The London *Times* of 3 October 1961 carried a column, by 'A Correspondent', entitled 'Sir Winston's Quotation'. The subheading ran: 'How the author of two elusive lines was tracked down.' The author was looking back to the early 1950s, when he was 'a rather undistinguished member' of the Conservative Central Office staff. Winston Churchill, as Leader of the Opposition, wanted to use a quotation in a speech the following week, and verification was required.

The lines were:

> Is there no room for victories here,
> No field for deeds of fame?[23]

Central Office library had already confirmed that they did not appear in any of their dictionaries of quotations. The only possible clue was that they had been a favourite quotation of 'a former Liberal friend, now long dead'. This, as was to become clear, was the Liberal politician and author Charles Masterman (1873–1927), who, according to the *Oxford Dictionary of National Biography*, had established 'something of a rapport' with Churchill. His widow, the formidable-sounding Lucy Masterman (according to *ODNB*, she had a 'toughness' denied to her husband), was still alive, but an approach to her resulted in the researcher's having the door shut in his face, with the information that she knew nothing about it at all, and in any case did not approve of many of the Conservative Party's current policies 'on *quite* a number of questions'.

Recourse to standard methods of research was still proving fruitless, with 'an information bureau', the British Museum Library, and the Poetry Society all having been invoked without success. 'But none of us got any results at all, and soon the time came when I was asked tentatively: did I think that perhaps Mr Churchill had got the quotation *wrong*?' Unable to believe this (past experience showing that Churchill's 'memory in matters of this sort was absolutely infallible'), the researcher finally decided that he had reached a dead end. 'I reluctantly decided that there was nothing more I personally could do. If the information bureau, the British Museum Library and the Poetry Society were all baffled, what hope was there for me? The job was out of my class.' He had also effectively run out of time—it was now Saturday, and the speech was to be delivered on Monday. He describes how, with time 'hanging heavily' on his hands, he picked up the previous day's Hansard. Parliament had recently reconvened, and he leafed through the Debate on the Address, noting a Labour Party member 'perorating in a dozen or so lines of poetry'. He could, he decided, skip that—but as he still had time before he went home, he glanced at it. What follows is an excellent description of how a sought-for wording can suddenly leap out of the page even when you are not consciously looking for it. 'For want of anything better to do, or perhaps because poetry was so much in the front of my subconscious mind—I glanced at it ... glanced—and suddenly sat up very sharply. For there—there, right in the middle of the quotation—were the two missing lines.'

Checking quickly, he ascertained that the author's name (William Watson) was given, and that Churchill appeared to have quoted correctly. However, the lines had just been quoted in the House—did that matter? Higher authority, to whom he referred the question, confirmed that it did not, and he should get it checked. Accordingly, he 'got busy in the public library at home'.

> By three o'clock, the answer had been telephoned to Chartwell. And Hansard records how, two days later, a second graceful tribute was paid in Parliament to 'the poet and teacher' [i.e. the poet William Watson] and suitable acknowledgements made to Mr Leslie Hale, the Labour MP for Oldham West, who had done more to help the Conservative Party Organization the previous week than perhaps he ever knew.[24]

The whole story is an excellent evocation of the reality, in pre-Internet days, of the way in which a well-planned systematic search (including, of course, the consultation of dictionaries of quotations) could prove fruitless.

Dangers Online

Since 2007, the United States Postal Service has issued 'forever stamps'—that is, first-class stamps that retain their face value even if the cost of first-class postage rises. A number of them have been issued as commemorative stamps. In 2015, a number of celebrities (real and fictional) were commemorated in this way, including Maya Angelou, Ingrid Bergman, Charlie Brown, and Paul Newman. Suitably enough, the Maya Angelou stamp, as well as showing her, included a quotation supposedly from her work. Less happily, it swiftly became known that the words in question, 'A bird doesn't sing because it has an answer, it sings because it has a song', were in fact the work of another writer (see Figure 8).

The prospective issue of the stamp (on 7 April 2015) was announced in the previous February, when the design was first unveiled. However, shortly before it formally appeared, the *Washington Post* carried a report under the subhead: 'Maya Angelou's new stamp uses a quote that may not be entirely hers.' The columnist, Lonnae O'Neal, recounted how an academic admirer of Maya Angelou's work, Jabari Asim, had been pleased and excited by the news, 'until he read the quote on the Angelou stamp'.

The *Washington Post* article notes that Professor Asim 'had seen the quote attributed to Angelou on social media but was highly sceptical. The Internet is full of misattributions. But the Postal Service?'[25] To check the provenance, he reached for a compilation of quotations on which he knew he could rely. This was not the

Figure 8. 'Forever' stamp issued in 2015 in honour of Maya Angelou with a mistaken attribution.

Oxford Dictionary of Quotations, Bartlett, or *The Yale Book of Quotations* (none of which in fact carries the quotation); it was his own note-book of quotations ('anything that appeals to me or resonates with me', as he explained), which he had admirably compiled over the course of eighteen years. He knew that the quotation would be there, and it was, under the name of the poet and children's author Joan Walsh Anglund.[26] It was certainly possible to find public instances of the attribution to Angelou. In 2013, for example, President Obama had included it in a speech.[27] More compellingly, Angelou herself had used the words in a blog post of 2013, when discussing her 1969 autobiography *I Know Why the Caged Bird Sings.* Usages like this probably helped tip the balance. The USPS gave a statement to the *Washington Post* in which their spokesman said: 'Maya Angelou was widely quoted as saying, "A bird doesn't sing because it has an answer, it sings because it has a song." There are numerous references in books, magazines, blogs and on the internet crediting Angelou with having said it as well.' In the resulting furore, they refused to reissue the stamp with a more appropriate quotation, taking their stand on the point that 'the sentence had great meaning for her, and she is publicly identified with its popularity'.[28] Joan Walsh Anglund herself, who might have been expected to object, took the news with generosity, saying: 'I think it easily happens sometimes that people hear something, and it's kind of going into your subconscious and you don't realize it.'

There is an interesting question here as to how far someone can justifiably be expected to go in checking provenance. In some ways, this was a mistake waiting to happen. There was evidence of wide public acceptance of the attribution to Angelou, including a comparatively high-profile citation that went unchallenged, and an actual use by the supposed author. Checking in major dictionaries of quotations would not have given any help. A private person (perhaps someone seeking a quotation for a speech) might have concluded that the attribution to Angelou was safe enough, although there are enough clues to provoke suspicion. If the saying had really been one closely associated with the title of Angelou's famous book, there ought to have been earlier evidence for the link. A chronological gap of over forty years is worrying. In fact, if an online search for 'a bird doesn't sing because it has an answer' is carried out, filtered by date, the Anglund reference comes up. And, even more importantly, the title of I Know Why the Caged Bird Sings is itself a direct quotation from an earlier poet of significance to Angelou. The poet Paul Laurence Dunbar (1872–1906) is described in The American National Biography as 'the first black American author to be able to support himself solely as a result of his writing'. In 1899 he published a collection of poems that included 'Sympathy'. The final verse runs:

> I know why the caged bird sings, ah me
> When his wing is bruised and his bosom sore—
> When he beats the bars, and he would be free;
> It is not a carol of joy or glee,
> But a prayer he sends from his heart's deep core,
> But a plea, that upward to heaven he flings—
> I know why the caged bird sings.[29]

In turn, the image can be linked back to the seventeenth century in the work of the English dramatist John Webster, and the line: 'We think caged birds sing, when indeed they cry.'[30]

More seriously, though, this attribution was not for a speech or ephemeral publication; it was for a commemorative stamp honouring Maya Angelou. The attribution should have been solid. 'Numerous' current references are not enough, since it is all too likely that they will reflect one another. This is where the authority of the traditional dictionary, or indeed a careful personal compilation such as Professor Asim's, comes into play.

The whole episode, of course, is likely to have its impact on dictionaries of quotations in turn, by justifying its inclusion in future editions. Bartlett, The Yale Book of Quotations, and the Oxford Dictionary of Quotations already have the quotations from Webster and Dunbar, with a reference to Angelou's title. I would now expect, for instance, that the next edition of the Oxford Dictionary of Quotations would include 'a bird doesn't sing because it has an answer, it sings because it has a song' under Anglund, with a note to indicate the popular (though erroneous) attribution to Angelou. Meanwhile this particular story stands as testimony to the dangers and the advantages of the Internet as a source. On the debit side, it is dangerously easy for a misattribution to establish itself. On the credit side, for those who look it is also possible to run a correct attribution to earth.

CHAPTER 3

THE WORLD OF QUOTATIONS

From the most serious and scholarly level to the most popular (inspirational and motivational quotes on mugs and personal websites), quotation is used to appeal to authority or to highlight a chosen saying to amuse or inspire. Quotations made with conscious reference ('as X famously said') often shed light on the social and cultural history of a particular period. Sources of this kind are often adduced for the values they represent. As Antony Jay wrote with his customary wit: 'In mobilizing support for a project or policy it is especially agreeable to be able to call upon the distinguished dead; their distinction adds intellectual weight and moral force to the argument, and their death makes it impossible to appear on television later and say that they meant something completely different.'[1] There is a serious point behind Dorothy Parker's light-hearted 'we all assume that Oscar said it'.[2]

There have always been favourite names to adduce in attribution. Traditionally Mark Twain and George Bernard Shaw have been preferred as sources for a pithy comment, and Einstein is now frequently called on. In recent years, the appeal of Mahatma Gandhi's principle of non-violent protest against civil and political wrongs has seen him increasingly favoured as a name to invoke, and as a result the number of apocryphal or unverified quotations attributed to him has increased. 'An eye for an eye makes the whole world blind' is likely today to be introduced with the words 'as Gandhi said'. 'The weak never can forgive. Forgiveness is the attribute of the strong' (reported in *Young India*, 2 April 1931) is one of the genuine Gandhi quotations added to the latest edition of the *Oxford Dictionary of Quotations*. 'First they ignore you. Then they laugh at you. Then they fight you. Then you win' is a modern saying that is now frequently misattributed to him.[3]

We may quote seamlessly, incorporating the words of another without acknowledgement into what we say or write, or we may compile a list of motivational quotations for personal online use. On some occasions it is demonstrable that it is the quotation itself, rather than the identity of its originator, that has caught the public imagination, and indeed the resonance of a particular name often decreases with time. When David Hume or Lord Chesterfield in the eighteenth century quoted the Cardinal de Retz, there was a reasonable assumption that the Machiavellian prelate of the Fronde would be a known figure to the reader, adding a context to what was being quoted. Quotations from de Retz today are more likely to have gained a place through their own merits rather than through authorship. In other instances, a quotation may be so inextricably linked with a particular event that it provides an allusive reference to it.

Some quotations, paradoxically, are almost too familiar to be recognized as quotations—they have become as much a part of the general vocabulary as any other idiom, and may appear in dictionaries as defined lexical items. Shakespeare is a key instance. It is a truism that Shakespeare's words are embedded in the language. Although it is now recognized that he may have been responsible for fewer coinages than once was thought, there are still a rich variety of phrases and other expressions that ultimately derive from his plays—from 'a rose by any other name' and 'the primrose path' to 'the winter of our discontent' and 'the witching hour'. Some are direct quotations, and others show some language change, so that 'method in one's madness' can be traced to Polonius' comment on Hamlet: 'If this be madness, yet there's method in it.'

Established quotations can generate phrases and sayings. There are, however, instances of traffic going the other way, when what was originally an expression of common wisdom achieves the status of an attributed quotation. When Gore Vidal died in 2012, Peter Lewis published a personal tribute in the *Mail Online* under the heading: 'Dying? As my friend Gore Vidal said, it's a good career move.' Within the body of the article, he noted that Vidal had 'famously' used the words on Truman Capote's death (Capote had died in 1984).[4] The quip is widely known, and Vidal's own account gives an interesting picture of how words may move from the private to the public sphere. Vidal was in Ravello when Capote died, and Jason Epstein, his editor at Random House, told him the news by phone. 'I said "Good career move." I said nothing to the press. But Jason chattered. I was much quoted.'[5]

There is a second tier to this: Vidal did not coin the saying, and it was not originally said about Capote. It turns up in a *Washington Post* column of November 1982, this time with Elvis Presley as the subject. Giving the view that 'being dead makes stars bigger than ever', the columnist writes: 'As the Hollywood agent is supposed to have said when Elvis Presley died, "Good career move." '[6]

Quote Investigator has traced this back to *Esquire*, 1 (1978), and an article by Peter Bogdanovich, 'The Murder of Sal Mineo'.[7] The form here is slightly different, with 'smart' replacing 'good': 'A Hollywood cynic was heard to call Presley's death a smart career move.'

It seems probable that, rather than being a unique coinage, 'good career move' is actually the kind of saying that might be applied by anyone of cynical turn of mind: its roots are in common wisdom rather than individual thought. The phrase itself can be traced back to the first half of the 1970s, so it was to hand for anyone wanting to comment on the particular circumstance. And the idea of humorously connecting death with improvement goes back much further. The British short-story writer 'Saki' (H. H. Munro, 1870–1916) used it in *Beasts and SuperBeasts* (1914). The young man-about-town Clovis Sangrail, considering an unloved acquaintance, says judiciously that 'Waldo is one of those people who would be enormously improved by death'. However, the employment of the phrase by Vidal appears to have personalized it: usage today is likely to include a reference to Gore Vidal or Truman Capote.

Significant Names

Association with a famous name can invest a quotation with lasting resonance. Quotations of this kind are often cited explicitly. On 28 March 2016, a *Boston Globe* columnist wrote a piece under the heading: 'In the election, our "better angels" will prevail.' The column was a critique of Donald Trump as a presidential campaigner. The columnist, Alex Beam, went on to explain his assumption (incorrect, as it turned out) that in the end the American people would reject Trump's appeal to their worst instincts: 'To steal a line from a friend of mine, we are a "better angels" country.' He then gave the original derivation of the phrase, from Abraham Lincoln's first Inaugural Address: 'The mystic chords of memory, stretching from every battlefield and patriot grave to every living heart and hearthstone all over this broad land, will yet swell the chorus of the Union when again touched, as surely they will be, by the better angels of our nature.'[8] This address was given just over a month before the first shots fired at Fort Sumter, on 12 April 1861, signalled the start of the Civil War. Beam points out that in the shorter term Lincoln was wrong. 'No angels descended from heaven to spare Americans the loss of 620,000 lives on the battlefield during the ensuing four years of combat.' Lincoln himself was to be assassinated just after the end of the war, on 14 April 1865. However, Beam asserts the view that in the longer term Americans have typically proved more likely to 'opt for a nebulous, uplifting promise of "hope and change" over more realistic policy promises' (let alone frightening and downbeat predictions). As he says, considering the better angels invoked by Lincoln, 'and yet the phrase stays with us'.

It has certainly stayed with a number of American presidents, or possibly their speech-writers. Those who have quoted the phrase include Herbert Hoover in 1931, Richard Nixon in his Inaugural Address of 1969 ('When we listen to the better angels of our nature, we find that they celebrate the simple things'), and Bill Clinton in his Christmas radio message of 1993 ('Part of the miracle of this season is that each of us can hear what Abraham Lincoln called "the better angels of our nature"'). The better angels were even referenced in relation to a fictional president, Jed Bartlett, in the first series of *The West Wing*. In one episode, the speech-writer Toby comments to the president: 'In a battle between a president's demons and his better angels, for the first time in a long time, I think we might have ourselves a fair fight.'[9] Overall, the 'better angels of our nature' can be seen as an example of what has been described by the linguist Frank Austermühl in the following passage:

> One of the consequences of the intertextual nature of presidential discourse is that certain passages from presidential speeches take on a life of their own. Key sections enter the nation's collective

discursive memory, and, as a staple element of presidential discourse, these quotations then combine to form a seemingly perpetual intertextual chain.[10]

Austermühl goes on to suggest that 'Lincoln's famous line "the last best hope of earth"' (from Lincoln's 1862 Annual Message to Congress) is probably the most famous example of this particular genre, and references Franklin Roosevelt, Eisenhower, Reagan, and the two Bushes in support. While a search made through Ngram Viewer to compare the popularity of the two over time suggests that the 'better angels' may yet have a slight edge, 'the last best hope' still makes a strong showing. It was invoked, for instance, in January 2017, in Rex Tillerson's opening statement to the Senate's Secretary of State hearings when he said: 'Abraham Lincoln declared that America is the "last best hope of Earth". Our moral light must not go out if we are to remain an agent of freedom for mankind.'[11]

Politics is always a rich area for quotations associated with particular figures—even if the words are not original coinages. The history of the expression 'kinder, gentler politics', now widely regarded as the coinage of the Labour leader Jeremy Corbyn, is instructive. The phrase is generally said to have come from Corbyn's first speech as Leader to the Labour Party conference, 29 September 2015. However, when the text of the speech is examined, this particular wording does not appear, although 'kinder' is found seven times (and gentle/gentler not at all). We have:

> Politics that's kinder, more inclusive.
> … the kinder politics we are pursuing
> … a kinder politics, a more caring society

... a kinder politics and a more caring society
... a kinder more caring politics
... that kinder more caring world
Let us build a kinder politics, a more caring society.

The key qualifiers, clearly, were 'kinder' and '(more) caring'. How then did the version 'kinder, gentler politics' establish itself, and how early can it be found?

One very early usage appears in an article by Mick Hume of 1 October 2015. The article (borrowing from Dylan Thomas) was entitled 'Do Not Go Gentle into that Good Night', and the first sentence read 'Labour leader Jeremy Corbyn made headlines calling for a "kinder, gentler" politics in his first big conference speech.'[12] Hume, who was not wholly uncritical of the approach, asked rhetorically: 'Who could disagree with the notion of nicer, gentler political debate?' He then went on to reiterate the supposed quotation: 'Nobody might want to celebrate rudeness or roughhouse tactics for their own sake. But anybody who wants to take seriously Corbyn's supposed support for "real debate" and "straight talking" will need to trample on his notion of kinder, gentler politics.' The previous day, Michael White's Labour conference diary in the *Guardian* had carried the comment: 'It may be a "kinder, gentler" Labour party in the future, as the leader promises—but business is business.'[13]

On the actual day of the conference speech, the *Guardian* website had a round-up of opinions from a panel of commentators, with individual assessments of what they saw as the key points of Corbyn's speech.[14] This provided a couple of near-quotes and paraphrases, with Matthew d'Ancona interestingly linking the wording with a quote from modern American politics. As he wrote: 'Just as George Bush Sr promised a "kinder, gentler nation" in 1988, so this Labour leader demanded "a kinder, more caring politics".' Polly Toynbee characterized Jeremy Corbyn as 'a nice man promising a kinder, gentler, more caring politics'. In short, it looks very much as though 'gentler' was introduced as a paraphrase rather than a direct quotation—perhaps helped, as Matthew d'Ancona pointed out, by echoes of the speech by George Bush Senior when accepting the presidential nomination of the Republican Party, 18 August 1988: 'I want a kinder and gentler nation.'

How swiftly, then, did 'kinder, gentler politics' establish itself as a quotation? Interestingly, many of the earlier uses seem to have been ironic. 'Where would the new kinder, gentler politics be without Ken Livingstone?' asked the journalist Marina Hyde rhetorically in the *Guardian*, 27 November 2015. A *Daily Telegraph* column of 2 December 2015 was headed: 'So much for your "kinder, gentler" politics, Jeremy.' There is also some evidence that 'kinder' was the qualifier that really made an impression. A wry allusion was made by Alan Johnson in a House of Commons debate on ISIL in Syria, 2 December 2015, when specific military action was contemplated: 'I find this decision as difficult to make as anyone. Frankly, I wish I had the self-righteous certitude of the finger-jabbing representatives of our new and kinder type of politics, who will no doubt soon be contacting those of us who support the motion tonight.'

Further usages tend to appear in the context of commentators surveying the scene and discerning a form of politics that seems neither kind nor gentle. However, in July 2016, Jeremy Corbyn was formally challenged for the leadership of the Labour Party. In the speech that launched his campaign to retain his position he spoke of 'laying the ground for a kinder, gentler politics that respects those unable to work, that treats disabled people with dignity'. Adding that he wanted to pay tribute to the Shadow Chancellor,

John McDonnell, he commented that 'someone said of him the other day: "He does the honest, straight-talking politics, but the kinder, gentler stuff is still work in progress."' The dual effect of the initial use of 'kinder, gentler politics' with the tongue-in-cheek endorsement of McDonnell effectively reclaims as a positive use what is now widely likely to be understood as a Corbyn coinage. And when the Labour leadership challenger Owen Smith apologized for his choice of language in expressing the wish that Labour should 'smash' the new prime minister, Theresa May, 'back on her heels', a spokesman for Jeremy Corbyn publicly deplored this 'aggressive' language with the reproachful comment: 'Jeremy has consistently called for a kinder, gentler politics. We should all reflect that in our political language.'[15]

On occasion, the selection of a quotation from a particular person can pose difficulties because of a view now taken of the person being quoted. The British journalist Martin Bell campaigned as an Independent in the general election of 1997. He won the seat of Tatton, and the scale of the victory was held to stand out even in a night when Labour won by a landslide, and many 'safe' Conservative seats changed hands. As one political commentator wrote next day:

> The other result which punctuated the night with special emotion came at 2.45 from Tatton, when Martin Bell's staggering 11,000 majority was announced. It was greeted by Bell with his trademark stoicism, but also with a new-found assurance. 'We are the people of England, and we have not spoken yet,' he said, quoting Chesterton, but pointing out that this was no longer true. The people of England had spoken.[16]

Martin Bell's choice of quotation had been deliberate, as he showed in his 2009 memoir revisiting the expenses scandal that had galvanized him to stand for parliament:

We, so martial and imperial abroad ... have proved at home to be a quiet, deferential, shoulder-shrugging people even in the face of the most dreadful abuses of power. We lowered our pikestaffs and went off to the pub. The great upheaval never actually happened. G. K. Chesterton caught this exactly in his poem 'The Secret People', which I quoted extensively in the Tatton campaign of 1997.[17]

However, Chesterton's vision of a diminished country in which the 'last, sad squires ride slowly towards the sea' is not necessarily seen as a positive image. Bell clearly took the lines as emblematic of people denied the voice they should have had, but they could be taken as signifying deliberate exclusivity. The point of view was expressed by the singer-songwriter and activist Billy Bragg, when interviewed three years later. The article, describing Bragg's rejection of Bell's quotation, calls Chesterton's line 'the anthem of silent-majority Little Englanderism', and quotes Bragg as saying that the poem is 'almost fascist in its content'. Bragg continued: 'When he quoted that I thought, Martin, you've got to *read* this poem. These squires who ride off towards the sea—these were the guys in their petrol tankers. They weren't doing it because they were trying to make a better society. It was pure self-interest.'[18] Bell's emphasis was on the words: Chesterton's name was there in acknowledgement, but not given any particular significance.

Chesterton's words are still frequently quoted. In 2005, the journalist Patrick Wright considered the contexts in which they are likely to be used. His *Guardian* column concluded:

Favoured by fox-hunting militants, they have also appeared on the banners of Countryside Alliance marchers: brandished as the slogan of a rural population considered to be oppressed by the values of the urban majority and a Labour government that has no respect for rural traditions. They have been recited by the 'Campaign for an

English Parliament' and also by the UK Independence party, for whom Chesterton's 'secret people' are patriots oppressed by the remote decision of the European Community.[19]

More recently, in April 2016, Timothy Garton Ash considered their continuing popularity. Referring to an essay by David Marquand in the *New Statesman*, he repeats Marquand's assertion that 'the Welsh word for England means "the lost land"—lost to the Celts, that is, when the Anglo-Saxons drove them out.' He then takes that idea forward to link with the Chesterton lines: 'The strange thing is that England is also something of a lost land for the English. Again and again, people quote G. K. Chesterton's poem about the "secret people" of England who "have not spoken yet".'[20]

Even more recently, the journalist Andrew Marr has testified to the poem's relevance (and place in his own vocabulary of quotations), writing in the aftermath of the Brexit vote in favour of leaving the European Union. Under a title ('The Biggest Blunder of them All') that made clear his own view of the outcome, he wrote: 'As dawn broke on Friday morning and I turned over in bed to grab my phone and Twitter, I thought immediately of G. K. Chesterton's poem from 1915, about the secret people of England.'[21] Having quoted a full verse beginning with the couplet:

> Smile at us, pay us, pass us; but do not quite forget.
> For we are the people of England, that never have spoken yet.

and ending with the line:

> Only you do not know us. For we have not spoken yet.

he concluded: 'Well, they have spoken now.'

Marr is aware of the ambivalent nature of his chosen quotation. He is careful to note that this 'great democratic moment' was accomplished peacefully and with a majority of well over a million—something that 'sets it aside from Chesterton's vision, which moves on from benign, bucolic defiance to outright anti-Semitism and warnings of blood-drenched revolution'. But, with the broader context deliberately excised, the chosen words remain a highly effective vehicle for conveying a startling political reality: a moment when an apparently disregarded electorate rejected the received wisdom of the political class. As Marr concludes, with an echo of the lines with which he started, 'It has been a very British revolution, accomplished through the ballot box and after a great deal of nonsense spoken on all sides. The plain people of England, mainly, have spoken at last and their voice has blown over not just a constitutional link with the European continent but also almost the entire political class.'

Another example of a name from an earlier period felt to have toxic associations was demonstrated in May 2007 when a US Congressman quoted the Confederate general Nathan Bedford Forrest's supposed 'Git thar fustest with the mostest.' In May 2007, Representative Ted Poe was arguing on the house floor for funds for military action in Iraq. He said: 'Congress needs to quit talking about supporting the troops, and put our money where our mouths seem to be. Nathan Bedford Forrest, successful Confederate general, said it best about winning and victory and the means to do so. He said, "Git thar fustest with the mostest."' The words attributed to Forrest (actually a popular version of his advice 'Get there first with the most men') were certainly apposite, and might have been seen as helpful to the argument. However, because of Forrest's own history (following the Civil War he became First Grand Wizard of the Klu Klux Klan), the citation generated outrage at the source rather than making a telling point. It is, however, worth noting that the expression is not always off limits. In February 2013, it appeared in *Time* magazine in an article on Pentagon budget cuts. Discussing the Defense Secretary's protest that the cuts would compromise America's ability to respond to crises, the journalist wrote: 'Of course, not everybody at the Pentagon sees it that way. Sure, money is always better when your mission is to "git thar fustest with the mostest." But there are those outliers who see austerity as a bracing tonic.'[22] Possibly the key difference here is that there was no name check, let alone an approving one. The expression is employed much more as an instance of common wisdom, and in the following year it was cited in that way (by the same journalist) as 'an old military truism'.[23] It may also be found in another context, attributed to another author. A column from *Chess News* of 28 December 2008 has the words as a heading. Below, the text describes it as a 'rather substantial quote from Frank Marshall', which 'could easily sum up his entire approach to chess'. Towards the end of his life the American chess champion Frank Marshall (1877–1944) published an autobiography entitled *My Fifty Years of Chess* (New York: Horowitz and Harkness, 1942). In it, he advises that 'in gambit openings the cardinal rule for each player is to "Git thar fustest with the mostest men"'. It seems clear in this instance that it was the approving citation of Forrest's name that aroused protest, rather than any specific problem with the adage.

Echoes of the Past

Sometimes a quotation is chosen because the circumstances in which it was originated appear to be strikingly echoed by the events of another time. This was notably evidenced in 2015 by the American Dialect Association's announcement of its Word of the Year, which included a category for 'Most Notable Hashtag'. One of the listings was for the hashtag *#JeSuisParis*.

'Je suis Paris' had emerged into the public domain in the aftermath of the terrorist outrages in Paris in November 2015. It was soon carried by English-language newspapers: the *Irish Independent* website of 14 November 2015 carried a heading *'Je suis Paris*: We Stand with the People of France'. The column concluded: 'All those who believe in freedom must declare, "Je suis Paris."' In Britain, the *Sun* newspaper ran a headline reading 'Je suis Paris: World Unites with France'.[24] The column below linked the slogan to one adopted after an earlier attack, saying: '*"Je suis Paris"*—I Am Paris—echoes the "Je Suis Charlie" slogan after January's *Charlie Hebdo* shootings in Paris.' A few days later it was announced that the reigning French football champions, Paris Saint-Germain, would wear shirts with the slogan 'Je suis Paris' to honour the victims of the attacks (see Figure 9). The associated hashtag took off: in December 2015 Twitter announced it as one of the most popular hashtags of the year.[25]

What may not have been clear to the English-speaking world, however, was just how far the words 'Je suis Paris' went back. In November 1870, when Paris was under siege by the Prussian army, *Le Figaro* carried a eulogy to the city, beginning 'Je suis Paris, la reine des cités', and signed 'Baron de L. …, Capitaine de garde mobile.'[26] This prose poem so impressed the composer César Franck, that he set it to music in 'Je Suis Paris, ode patriotique pour voix avec orchestre'—ensuring the longevity of the opening words. The first performance, in fact, marked another significant moment of French history, as evidenced by an article on Franck published in November 1918:

Figure 9. Paris Saint-Germain football players in 'Je Suis Paris' shirts.

It needed this War even for his patriotic Ode to Paris to come to light. Composed in a burst of enthusiasm during the Siege of Paris in the war of 1870, it was performed for the first time last year before a vast throng stirred to their very depths as the voice of the tenor rang out 'Je Suis Paris—la Reine des cités'—and the great orchestra proclaimed the invincible spirit of the French people even in their darkest hour of adversity.[27]

Events of 1870 provided another key quotation for 2015. Following the November terrorist attacks in Paris, the journal *Voice of America* carried a piece by Lisa Bryant, in which she described how flowers and notes were being left along the Rue de la Fontaine du Roi, where the shootings had taken place. She described interviewing one man who had laid such tributes, including some words of the nineteenth-century writer Victor Hugo. 'Asked for an example, he quoted from Hugo's *Deeds and Words*, referring to the 1870 siege of Paris during the Franco-Prussian war: "Paris is the sacred city—who attacks Paris attacks the entire human race."[28] At the outbreak of the Franco-Prussian War, Victor Hugo had been living in exile for many years. He returned to France on the fall of Napoleon III, and arrived in Paris on 5 September 1870. The following passage comes from his address to the crowd at the Gare du Nord: 'To save Paris is more than to save France, it is to save the world. Paris is the very centre of humanity. Paris is the sacred city. Who attacks Paris attacks in mass the entire human race. Paris is the capital of civilization. And do you know why Paris is the city of civilization? It is because Paris is the city of revolution.'[29] The words have become iconic. In January 2016, ceremonies were held in Paris to commemorate the anniversary of the *Charlie Hebdo* shootings (7 January 2015) and the November attacks. The commemoration culminated on 10 January 2016 with a rally on the Place de la République, and as part of the proceedings two drama students read out Hugo's speech.

It is hardly surprising that *#JeSuisParis* overtook both the earlier *#PrayforParis* and *#JeSuisCharlie* in popularity. It links back to a famous speech, made at a significant moment, which evoked the concept of Paris under attack but refusing to be defeated.

Famous Allusions

'Famous' quotations often imprint themselves on the public consciousness, often to the degree that they establish a formulation that can be used allusively. If the reference is not picked up, it does not compromise the essential meaning, but recognition can add a further dimension. In the case of 'Patriotism is not enough', the words of the British nurse Edith Cavell (1865–1915) on the eve of her execution by the Germans for helping Allied soldiers escape from Belgium, there is evidence not only of the quotation's ultimate success, but of its earlier adoption into the public vocabulary.

In May 2016, the *New Statesman* magazine carried an article by the British Labour politician Chuka Umunna entitled 'Tolerance is not enough: Against the Trumpification of Politics'. In it he argued not that what he called the 'British spirit of "tolerance"' was not in itself desirable, but that for a just society other positive qualities were also required. This usage is in line with the original quotation on which his heading was surely modelled. The words became emblematic: marking the centenary of her death in October 2016, the *Docklands and East London Advertiser* carried an article under the heading: '"Patriotism is not Enough"—why we Remember Edith Cavell's Execution 100 Years on.'[30]

A key part of the reason why, of course, has been the way in which the words have been kept in the public eye. To take one example, *The Times* of 23 October 1915 had carried an account by the British Chaplain at Brussels who had been allowed to visit Edith Cavell on the night before her execution. He reported her words to him, including the passage: 'They have all been very kind to me here. But this I would say, standing, as I do, in view of God and eternity. I realize that patriotism is not enough. I must have no hatred or bitterness towards anyone.' The passage became the source of her 'famous last words', much quoted in 2015, the centenary year of her death. As David Piper's *Companion Guide to London* puts it, 'in her dying she welded herself into the living conscience of English history with four words, *Patriotism is not enough*'.[31] Piper was writing about the Edith Cavell memorial, by Sir George Frampton, which stands north-east of Trafalgar Square, and which has these words engraved on its plinth (see

Figure 10. Monument to Edith Cavell including the words 'Patriotism is not enough'.

Figure 10). In Virginia Woolf's novel *The Years*, published in 1937, the statue and its inscription were well enough known to be referred to elliptically. Eleanor, with her friend Peggy, is driving past the memorial:

> 'The only fine thing that was said in the war,' she said aloud, reading the words cut on the pedestal.
> 'It didn't come to much,' said Peggy sharply.[32]

There is no question but that Woolf expected her readers to know the inscription. It is therefore the more surprising to realize that, despite their fame, they were not originally inscribed on the memorial when it was erected in 1920. As the *Times* account of the unveiling of the memorial by Queen Alexandra described it:

> There is a striking representation of the tall, graceful figure of the heroine, looking towards the south, and at the foot is the simple inscription:—'Edith Cavell, Brussels, Dawn, Oct. 12, 1915.' The words 'Humanity', 'Devotion', 'Fortitude', and 'Sacrifice' are inscribed on the four broad facias of the monument; and above these are the words 'For King and Country' and 'Faithful unto Death'.[33]

It is not that the key words had not already been used for a memorial. In 1916, the anniversary of her death had been marked by the unveiling of a memorial to her in the nurses' dining room at Shoreditch Infirmary, where she had been Assistant Matron between 1903 and 1906. The *Times* account, noting that the artist, Gordon M. Forsyth, had donated his services for free, added that other expenses were covered by local subscription. The memorial, an oil painting in three panels showing the figures of Faith, Hope, and Charity, with children, had a carved oak frame with an inscription. This read (in a slight variation from the known text): 'Patriotism is not enough. I must be free from hatred and bitterness.'[34]

In her 2004 account of the Frampton memorial, Sue Malvern discusses the critical reception of the memorial, quoting especially from the *Star* of 17 March 1920, which criticized the substitution of 'the conventional language of dull officialism for her moving message to the distracted earth is a wrong to her memory and a perversion of historic truth'. They added simply: 'Let it be undone.' Discussing the process by which the change was made, and the reasons why Cavell's 'last words' might have been considered controversial, she suggests that the statement 'patriotism is not enough, I must have no hatred or bitterness for anyone' is ambiguous. It could imply 'by omission that patriotic allegiance might necessitate enmity and resentment'.[35] Other contemporary critics included the essayist Arthur Clutton-Brock (1868–1924), who wrote in the *New Statesman*:

> There is a single and moving idea connected with her memory and expressed by herself when she was facing death. She said then: Patriotism is not enough—and she meant that she was dying, not for her country or as the enemy of any other country, but for mankind. If her memory is sacred to us those words of hers ought to be sacred: they ought to be the theme of her memorial and inscribed, if any words are inscribed, upon it.[36]

Clutton-Brock concluded that the omission of the words in favour of 'For King and Country' implied that 'we do not agree with her: we think that patriotism is enough and we have chosen to say so on a monument erected in her honour'. The writer John Middleton Murry was similarly disapproving, commenting: 'It demeans her great sacrifice to have replaced the solemn message of the heroine with words that may be found in any monumental mason's catalogue.'[37] George Bernard Shaw, writing a few years later on a much earlier national heroine, Joan of Arc, was even more severe. In his view:

> Her [Edith Cavell's] countrymen, seeing in this a good opportunity for lecturing the enemy on his intolerance, put up a statue to her, but took particular care not to inscribe on the pedestal 'Patriotism is not enough', for which omission, and the lie it implies, they will need Edith's intercession when they are themselves brought to judgment.[38]

Criticism was followed by a direct campaign, organized by the National Council of Women. They appealed to the Office of Works late in 1922. The campaign, despite some hostility, was successful. Malvern records that the Labour government approved the change in 1924. Interestingly from the point of view of quotational accuracy, the form chosen was approved as canonical by the Cavell family (who also added their support to the desirability of adding the inscription). The story is one that demonstrates the capacity of particular words to lodge themselves into the public conscious-ness, and perhaps the inability of 'dull officialism' to counteract the process, and its impact on language.

Careful Selection

At times, a very careful deliberate selection of words can be made from a longer passage, something that is illustrated by usage from the source of Bismarck's well-known phrase 'blood and iron'. Today, the expression is synonymous with repression, as evi-denced John McCain in the US Senate debating the apparent breakdown of a fragile ceasefire in Syria. The *Politico* website, not-ing that McCain was chairman of the Senate Armed Services Committee, and a longtime critic of what it described as the presi-dent's 'largely hands-off approach to Syria', quoted McCain as asserting: 'In the words of Mr Bismarck, "The issue will be decided by blood and iron."'[39]

'Blood and iron', in relation to the policy of unification of Germany based on military power, was used more than once by Bismarck, initially with the order of the nouns reversed. Speaking to the Prussian Assembly in September 1862, Bismarck had said: 'The great questions of the day will not be decided by speeches and resolutions of majorities—that was the great mistake from

1848 to 1849—but by iron and blood.' Over twenty years later, he revisited the same theme, addressing the Prussian House of Deputies, in January 1886: 'This policy cannot succeed through speeches, and shooting-matches, and songs; it can only be carried out through blood and iron.' However, it is the 1862 utterance in particular that has caught public attention: A. J. P. Taylor calls it 'his most famous sentence'. Before the now-familiar appellation of the 'Iron Chancellor', he was referred to as the 'man of blood and iron'—as, for example, in a report from Vienna in July 1864 by the *Times* correspondent on the unexpectedly low-key arrival there of the German Chancellor:

> A strong-willed and energetic statesman being a rarity in Germany, it was expected that many of the political quidnuncs of Vienna would go to the railway terminus to see, if not to welcome, the man 'of blood and iron'; but such was not the case ... few of the persons whom they [Bismarck and Baron Werther, who had gone to meet him] met in the streets turned to look at the man who by superior ability and force of will has succeeded in making Austria subservient to Prussia.[40]

'Blood and iron' was the form in which Bismarck's phrase became established in English, to the extent that a piece of propaganda published in London in 1914 was entitled: 'The German gospel of blood and iron. Germany's war mania. A collection of speeches and writings by the German emperor [and others].' 'Blood and iron' at that point was a phrase carrying a dangerous import, as it was in the years leading up to the Second World War. The *Times* of June 1938 reported on the speech given in Stockholm by Viscount Cecil of Chelwood, the former Lord Robert Cecil, as recipient of the Nobel Peace Prize.[41] His speech included the warning that 'again we see rising the idea that might is right, that mercy and tolerance are only symptoms of feebleness, and that the old conception of blood and iron is the only thing to trust'. It is interesting, therefore, that by the 1960s the source of Bismarck's original claim could be quoted to another German Chancellor with much less ominous associations. In August 1967, President Lyndon Johnson received Chancellor Kiesinger of West Germany at the White House.[42] At a formal dinner, the president proposed a toast—for which, as he indicated, some research had been done:

> While preparing this toast, Mr Chancellor, I asked an aide to find an appropriate phrase from an illustrious German leader. He came back a few minutes later with the following words of Bismarck: 'Not by speechifying and counting majorities are the great questions of the time to be solved ...' I stopped him right there. It was obvious that neither he nor Bismarck had very much experience in running for office.
>
> Borrowing a quotation from one of your great poets, Goethe, we shall proceed, Mr Chancellor, without haste—but without rest.[43]

By cutting off the aide, Johnson adroitly shifted the whole balance of Bismarck's sentence to reflect a different approach to electioneering—rather than advocating the exercise of power through military means. It would be interesting to know how many of his English-speaking hearers in 1967 recognized the truncated quotation. A Twitter source in 2010 quoted the shortened version among a list of positive and motivational quotations and sayings, and online evidence in 2016 suggests that it is still reasonably well known. Overall, it would seem that Bismarck's words no longer carry the aggressive context of the Chancellor's 'blood and iron' approach to political problems.

Choosing your Words

Quotations may be taken out of context, but not otherwise modi-fied. In other instances, key words and phrases are borrowed and adjusted to fit their new purpose. January 2016 marked the thirty-year anniversary of the 1986 *Challenger* disaster, when the US space shuttle *Challenger* was destroyed on take-off, and all its crew lost. The *Washington Post* marked the anniversary with a column headed: 'Exactly the right words, exactly the right way: Reagan's amazing Challenger disaster speech.'[44] The column went on to consider the address given (at very short notice) by Ronald Reagan in response to the tragedy. The text had been prepared by his speech-writer, Peggy Noonan, and in her memoirs she gave a detailed account of how the speech was composed. Her text incorporated two lines from 'High Flight' by the airman John Gillespie Magee (1922–41), published in 1943 after his death. The lines were 'Oh, I have slipped the surly bonds of earth' and 'Put out my hand and touched the face of God'. The passage in Reagan's address ran: 'We will never forget them, nor this last time we saw them this morning, as they prepared for the journey and waved goodbye and "slipped the surly bonds of earth" to "touch the face of God".'[45]

President Reagan's words had to be prepared in the shortest possible time—a challenge, but not necessarily a disadvantage. As Peggy Noonan's account clarified, 'the staffing process had no time to make it bad', although they had had to fight off an 'improve-ment' that would have read 'reach out and touch someone—touch the face of God.' It was apparently explained to the staffer who made this suggestion that 'you don't really change a quotation from a poem in this manner'.[46] The sureness of her perception is exemplified by the *Washington Post*'s endorsement thirty years later.

Reaching a Wider Public

Ronald Reagan's address following the loss of *Challenger* is probably one of his best-remembered speeches, and Peggy Noonan's reworking of Magee's lines have consequently been widely known from the first. By contrast, other quotations that may now be claimed as famous seemed to have reached a wider public much more slowly, sometimes by diverse paths. In 2014, on the death of the Duke of Marlborough, the *Telegraph*'s obituary included a quotation from Gladstone on the Churchill family:

> Yet even Queen Anne did not anticipate the grandeur and huge expense of Blenheim, and the house went on to become a financial burden to the Dukes of Marlborough for more than 300 years. The huge expense of maintaining the house often tempted them to desperate stratagems that did little for their reputation—or happiness. Gladstone famously remarked: 'There never was a Churchill from John of Marlborough down that had either morals or principles.'[47]

Examining how 'famous' this remark actually is can be enlightening. David Cannadine quoted it in his essay on the Churchill family, saying that 'Gladstone's harsh words of 1882 expressed the generally held late Victorian view'.[48] However, I have not to date found an instance of the words in any book before 1981, when the historian Roy Foster gave an account of them—and the circumstance in which they were spoken. In his biography of Lord Randolph, Foster describes how, in the early 1880s, Churchill's name was being canvassed as a possible party leader. However, not all responses to the idea were favourable. Apparently a young naval officer, at table with Gladstone, had suggested the possibility. Years later, Arthur Balfour asked the naval officer (now retired) to write down his recollections of Gladstone's reaction when as a young man he had suggested that Lord Randolph was a future leader of the Tory party: '[Gladstone] fixed me with his glittering, hawk-like eyes—"Never. God forbid that any great English party should be led by a Churchill! There never was a Churchill from John of Marlborough down that had either morals or principles." '[49]

There are two points of interest here. First, Gladstone's characterization of a whole family seems to have derived from his strong feeling about one member of it (Lord Randolph), and his unsuitability for the role of party leader, let alone prime minister. Secondly, and most importantly, the history of the quotation demonstrates by what convoluted paths 'famous' words may reach the public. The words were spoken by Gladstone on a private occasion in 1882, and apparently not committed to paper until 1913—and that, at the intervention of another person, Arthur Balfour. But the memorandum was not published, and it was nearly seventy years before the key words appeared in print, in Foster's life of Lord Randolph. It is of course possible, indeed probable, that Gladstone may have said something similar on other occasions, and that the words were known within society, but at present there does not seem to be any evidence for it.

Some 'familiar' quotations are initially best known within a particular subject area, but then reach out to a wider public, perhaps through the work of a particular writer. In March 2015, an article in *Universe Today* reporting on NASA'S airborne SOFIA observatory was headed: 'As it Turns out, we Really Are All Starstuff.'[50] The heading referenced a saying by the bestselling science writer Carl Sagan, discussing the nature of the cosmos: 'We are made of starstuff.' A year later to the day, the *Manchester*

Guardian reported on the witnessing by astronomers of a super-nova shockwave—the first time the phenomenon had been seen. At the end of the piece, Steve Howell, a Nasa scientist, was quoted, explaining that supernova explosions are the source of all heavy metals in the universe: 'Life exists because of supernovae.' The writer of the column summed up, in a way that clearly expected the *Guardian*'s readership to have some familiarity with what was to be quoted: 'That's not quite as poetic as the way US astronomer Carl Sagan famously put it: "The nitrogen in our DNA, the calcium in our teeth, the iron in our blood, the carbon in our apple pies were made in the interiors of collapsing stars. We are made of starstuff."'[51] The column concluded by noting that the findings had been accepted for publication in the *Astrophysical Journal*.

Carl Sagan was a bestselling science writer whose work was accessible to the non-scientist. The mathematician G. H. Hardy, on the other hand, while highly successful as a writer, addressed himself largely to the mathematical world. His *A Mathematician's Apology*, however, published in 1940, is a memoir that has a wider appeal, and one quotation from it now has a growing degree of public recognition. It relates to the essential creativity of mathematics: 'A mathematician, like a painter or a poet, is a maker of patterns.' It is possible to find this spread across the Internet today, and in 2015 it achieved another level of recognition, when a sculpture by Simon Periton, *The Alchemical Tree*, was installed as a piece of public art in the newly refurbished Radcliffe Observatory Quarter in Oxford (see Figure 11). The metal sculpture of an ash tree is adorned with strips of metal carrying selected quotations, one of which is Hardy's assertion. It seems likely that the Oxford tourist trail will in due time play its part in introducing this quotation about the nature of mathematics to the general public.

Figure 11. Simon Periton's sculpture of *The Alchemical Tree*, Radcliffe Observatory Quarter, Oxford.

The Latest Thing

One category of 'famous saying', of course, is the current coinage—
something that immediately garners public attention. One example,
early in 2017, was the formulation 'alternative facts' as used by
President Trump's spokeswoman Kellyanne Conway on 22 January
in an interview on *Meet the Press*. Questioned about estimates for
numbers watching the presidential inauguration, which differed
significantly from claims made by the White House Press Secretary
Sean Spicer, Conway said that Spicer was 'giving alternative facts
to that'. In the United States, the website for Merriam-Webster's
dictionaries maintains a 'Trending' list of terms that have been
looked up most frequently. Shortly after Ms Conway issued her
clarification, the website posted a note on 'fact' (defined as 'a piece
of information presented as having objective reality') saying that
the number of times the word had been looked up had 'spiked
dramatically' following the interview.[52]

It will now be interesting to see what longevity they turn out to
have—they could drop from sight, or survive as emblematic of an
administration's approach to the media. The most difficult thing
with recent coinages is to guess how long they will last. 'He would,
wouldn't he', referred to in the Introduction, was an arguably trite
way to imply that a denial in the circumstances was only to be
expected. But the high-profile nature of the circumstances fixed
the words in the public mind, and they passed into the wider
vocabulary as a phrase that at once admitted that a denial had
been made, and refused it any credence.

Personal Favourites

Not all quotations that come to light are from the area of public discourse. Contrastingly, some quotations are cited because they have been particularly meaningful to an individual rather than being widely known. In 2015, I was asked by an acquaintance if I could help in finding the source of a quotation. Some years ago, when after her grandfather's death the family were clearing up his papers, they found a piece of paper with what appeared to be lines from a poem written on it: 'Silently, unawares and unbelievably come all great things—the inroad of great love, the mist of death.' It was clearly significant to him, but no one recognized the lines—and, as his granddaughter commented, there was at that time (the 1990s) no facility for online searching. Possible authors were canvassed (the nineteenth-century Scottish poet and novelist George MacDonald had been one of his favourite writers), but no leads were found. Searching through dictionaries of quotations had proved fruitless. However, when his granddaughter and I happened to meet, she thought it was worth asking if I, as Editor of the *Oxford Dictionary of Quotations*, had ever come across it.

I had not, but it struck me at once as very suitable for online searching—a phrase like 'inroad of great love' makes a very distinctive string. A search of Google Books took me to a poem ('Picture of the Nativity in the Church of Krena in Chios') by C. A. Trypanis, which had first appeared in his collection *Pedasus* (1955), and which subsequently appeared in America in 1961 in a periodical devoted to modern Greek culture.[53] The first verse of the poem evokes a poorly painted picture of the Nativity (the angels have 'flat, clumsy wings') whose very banality prompts the question whether the 'unsuspecting infant' depicted can be 'He, who trampled upon death'. The last two lines of the poem run:

—Silently, unawares and unbelievably come all
Great things; the inroad of great love, the mist of death.

Constantine A. Trypanis (1909–93) was a poet and classical scholar, born in Chios, who became the Bywater and Sotheby Professor of Byzantine and Modern Greek Language and Literature at Oxford. When he died in 1993, Peter Levi's obituary of him opened: 'Constantine Trypanis was a poet in English who interested Eliot and by a long chalk the best medieval and modern Greek scholar of his generation.'[54] This, as my acquaintance said, all fitted in, as her grandfather had also been an Oxford classicist of that generation.

The whole story constitutes a nice example of how something that is in no sense a 'famous' quotation, or possibly even moderately well known beyond a particular area of scholarship, had clearly been of great significance to one particular person, and treasured. It also demonstrates how fortunate we are today to be able to search online—hoping, as happened in this case, that someone will have scanned or digitized an original that will lead us to the source of the quotation.

Echoing Phrases

This quotation had clearly been recorded because it was meaningful, but sometimes words can be retained simply through their resonance. In *Something of Myself* (1937), Rudyard Kipling recalled two loved (and lost) books of his childhood. 'One—blue and fat—described "nine white wolves" coming "over the wold" and stirred me to the deeps.'

The books remembered by Kipling have been identified: the 'nine white wolves' come from a poem set at the north pole. The key verse runs:

> And as one strode so bold,
> He saw a sight of fear,
> Nine white wolves came over the wold,
> And they were watching a deer.
>
> —'A North Pole Story'[55]

In this poem, a comparison is drawn between the deer, which, because it fears the wolves, becomes their prey, and the man, who looks them in the eye and survives. The poet's evocation of the scene impressed the young Rudyard, but he was presumably unaware (then and later) that, when Menella Bute Smedley wrote her poem, she was basing it on a famous and factual account of Arctic travel. The nine white wolves originally came from a story in the journal of the Scottish physician, naturalist, and Arctic explorer Sir John Richardson (1787–1865). As 'Dr Richardson', he accompanied Franklin on his expedition to look for the North-West Passage in 1819–22.[56] Franklin's published account of 1823 tells how Richardson encountered 'nine white wolves', initially hunting a deer, and later menacing himself.

Dr Richardson having the first watch, had gone to the summit of the hill, and remained seated contemplating the river that washed the precipice under his feet, long after dusk had hid distant objects from his view. His thoughts were, perhaps, far distant from the surrounding objects, when he was roused by an indistinct noise behind him, and on looking round, perceived that nine white wolves had arranged themselves in the form of a crescent, and were advancing, apparently with the intention of driving him into the river. On his rising up they halted, and when he advanced they made way for his passage down to the tents.[57]

The story was repeated in the *Annual Register* for 1823, and in the *Quarterly Review*'s account of Franklin's book.[58] It also found its way into a publication for children, *Arctic Travels* (1830), presented as a dialogue between the captain of a trading vessel, Captain Mackey, and William and Patrick Jones, the two sons of a Waterford merchant. However, for Kipling it was evidently the ring of the words of the 'nine white wolves' coming 'over the wold' that stayed with him, rather than any consideration of their literary antecedents.[59]

CHAPTER 4

THE PAROLE OF LITERARY MEN

According to Dr Johnson in 1781: 'Classical quotation is the parole of literary men the world over.'[1] From the Bible and Shakespeare, to Milton, Pope, and later writers, individual quotations from what are regarded as major literary sources have established themselves strongly in the language. Many, quoted across the centuries, have generated both phrases and sayings, contributing to the stock of what is now recognized as common wisdom. Many such phrases can be found as defined lemmas in lexical dictionaries. Others, which have not yet achieved that level of recognition, can be demonstrated to have a similar level of existence independent of their original source or context.

Despite the prevalence today of quotations from a plethora of modern and contemporary sources, what have traditionally been regarded as classic works and writers still hold their place.

Holy Writ

In *Begat* (2010), his study of the impact of the King James translation of the Bible on the English language, David Crystal considered the assertion that 'no book has had greater influence on the

English language'. He concluded that this claim did not hold in respect of the coinage of new words, or of stylistic innovation. It could, however, be justified if it were 'interpreted with reference to the number of innovative expressions in a single canonical work of literature'.[2] In the course of the book, he examines a total of 257 phrases such as 'fly in the ointment', 'thorn in the flesh', and 'the way of all flesh'. He demonstrates which of them originated with the Authorized Version, and which can be traced back to earlier translations ('salt of the earth', he points out, goes back to Tyndale's translation of the Bible[3]). In revealing that the King James Version can be seen as the originator in only a comparatively small group of items, he stresses the importance of the earlier translators. The King James Version did more than any other translation to fix expressions in the mind of the English-speaking public, but the 'myriad contributions' of Wycliffe, Tyndale, and many others need to be remembered. 'Their linguistic fingerprints are to be found in the pages of the King James Bible. They are an essential element in the story of how the English language was "begat".'

In considering the impact of the King James Version, Crystal provides evidence of varying translations in earlier versions of the Bible. For the purposes of this book, it is also of interest to ask which translations hold in modern versions, and which are so different as to be almost unrecognizable? But, as one anecdote attests, the poetic qualities of the King James Version may still have an appeal.

Quotations may be selected very specifically for a speech: the policy adviser Peter Hyman gives an account of doing so when working as a speech-writer for Tony Blair. He was working on the draft of the prime minister's main speech to the Labour Party conference of 2003, when Tony Blair said that he wanted a particular biblical quotation included. It was, he thought, from Proverbs, and said exactly what they wanted to say in the speech. The wording was along the lines of 'if we faint in the day of struggle we have little strength'.

In a passage that now has an extraordinarily dated feeling, Hyman describes a pre-Internet search for a wanted text. He begins by looking for 'the obligatory hotel bible', and discovers that 'Tony is almost spot on'. At Proverbs 24:10, he finds the words: 'If we faint when there's trouble then we have little strength.' However, Tony Blair wants it from a 'more poetic' version and suggests the King James Bible, something that Hyman finds a challenge—where will he get a King James Bible at 10 p.m. on a Monday night?

> I phone the only person I know will be working at this hour, the Number 10 Duty Clerk, the heroic person on duty through the night to take messages and sort out logistics for the Prime Minister at Number 10. He calls me back within the hour. 'If we faint in the day of adversity, our strength is small.' That's more poetic. Tony will like it.[4]

Clearly, Tony did: the key words appeared in the culminating section of his speech to the 2003 conference (although it is worth noting that Hyman has modernized the quotation slightly: what the Authorized Version actually has is 'If thou faint in the day of adversity, thy strength is small').

Today we are regularly told that the number of churchgoers is decreasing; a very small number of them indeed are likely to hear a lesson read from the Authorized Version of the Bible. To what degree in future will particular biblical phrases be recognized as being 'from the Bible'?[5]

Quoting Shakespeare

As a source of phrases that have become embedded in the language, Shakespeare has been regarded as only second to the Bible (see Figure 12). The point that many Shakespearean phrases had become part of the language was made a number of years ago by the critic Bernard Levin (1928–2004) in his piece 'You are Quoting Shakespeare'.[6] A reading of the passage by the actor Rob Brydon preceded the screened version of Kenneth Branagh's 2015 production of *The Winter's Tale*. The opening words run: 'If you cannot understand my argument, and declare "It's Greek to me", you are quoting Shakespeare'; it concludes: 'What the dickens! But me no buts!—it is all one to me, for you are quoting Shakespeare.' In between, phrases mentioned include 'if your wish is father to the

Figure 12. Goss china souvenir from Stratford-on-Avon, showing a cauldron decorated with the incantation of Macbeth's witches, 'Double, double, toil and trouble'.

thought', 'salad days', 'fool's paradise', 'bag and baggage', 'give the devil his due', 'cold comfort', 'at one fell swoop', 'without rhyme or reason', and 'dead as a doornail'. It is a most attractive piece of writing, and a number of the expressions cited are indeed a Shakespearean coinage—for example, 'at one fell swoop', Macduff's protesting cry at hearing of the murder of his wife and children at the hands of Macbeth. Others, however, such as 'fool's paradise' and 'without rhyme or reason', may be found in Shakespeare's writings, but were not originated by him. To take one particular example, 'tower of strength' had been used in the 1549 Book of Common Prayer in the Marriage Service: 'O Lord … Be unto them a tower of strength.' However, that does not invalidate Levin's main point: that a significant number of phrases will have been encountered in Shakespeare's plays. Whether or not Shakespeare was responsible for their coinage, they are now part of the general vocabulary, and likely to be used without the intention of invoking the characters of Cleopatra ('salad days') or Cicero ('Greek to me').

Shakespeare is widely quoted today. A random search online in February 2016 turned up a range of attributed items, including 'the course of true love never did run smooth', 'age cannot wither her, nor custom stale | Her infinite variety', and 'there are more things in heaven and earth, Horatio, | Than are dreamt of in your philosophy'. The *Church Times* of 19 February 2016 carried a sub-heading 'All Greek (or Latin) to me', and the answer to a clue in the *Times* Jumbo crossword of 13 February 2016 was 'eye of newt and toe of frog'. (The plays thus implicitly referenced are respectively *A Midsummer Night's Dream*, *Antony and Cleopatra*, *Hamlet*, *Julius Caesar*, and *Macbeth*—all well known and frequently performed.) A couple are quite clearly quotations, while the first could be understood as a piece of proverbial wisdom, as at a stretch could 'all Greek to me'. Even 'eye of newt and toe of frog' could be taken as an idiom, although it is clearly illuminated by being recognized as part of the Weird Sisters' recipe.

Well-known Shakespearean quotations may have freed themselves from their original context. In April 2016, just before Shakespeare's birthday, the online journal *Entrepeneur* published a list of '15 Inspirational Quotes on the 400th Anniversary of Shakespeare's Death'.[7] Among the quotations listed, the tongue-in-cheek advice given to Malvolio—'Be not afraid of greatness: Some are born great, some achieve greatness, and some have greatness thrust upon them'—was listed under the heading 'Identify Opportunity'. The list itself was said to encapsulate 'some of his [Shakespeare's] most memorable quotes about leadership, facing your fears and taking advantage of every opportunity that comes your way'—in other words, these are 'well-known words' with which the magazine's readers might be supposed to be familiar, and which will speak directly to their situation. They have also, significantly, become detached from their original context, when they were framed to delude the vainglorious Malvolio rather than encouraging appropriate aspiration.

These are all Shakespearean quotations for which a long usage trail can be demonstrated, and which can occur in a variety of contexts. In other cases, a quotation may have much more intermittent usage, and may also demonstrate much more specificity of use. In October 2013, the *Independent* reported on a forthcoming production of *Richard III*, the first major production since the remains of Richard were discovered under a Leicester car park. Archaeological investigation had revealed exactly how Richard was killed at the battle of Bosworth, and the stage fight would reflect it as accurately as possible. As the column reported:

The 'Crookback King' has been despatched on stages around the world for more than 400 years to Richmond's merciless cry: 'The day is ours, the bloody dog is dead.'

Now, for the first time since Shakespeare penned his masterpiece of Tudor propaganda, theatre audiences can witness the true—and no less brutal—circumstances of Richard III's demise on Bosworth Field.[8]

The quotation here is used in context to underline the violence of Richard's end: a direct quotation relating to the original circumstance. It cannot be claimed as one of the most popular quotations from the play: a comparison using NGram Viewer 'my kingdom for a horse', and indeed the line added by Colley Cibber in the eighteenth century, 'Richard's himself again!' demonstrates much wider usage for these phrases. Arguably, they are more susceptible of extended usage, but two very particular examples can be found for 'the bloody dog is dead.'

In the summer of 1942, the Nazi leader Reinhardt Heydrich was assassinated by Czech partisans. The *Central European Observer* of 12 June 1942, reporting on his death and the consequent savage reprisals, gave its account the headline: '"The Bloody Dog is Dead" (*Shakespeare—Richard III*)'—for once, an effectively literal use of a quotation. Three years later, there was a similar instance. The writer Thomas Mann, then living in America, described the 'daily hail of fantastic reports' of the summer of 1945. These included the capture and death of Mussolini, the Soviet flag flown from the Reichstag, and 'Hitler and Goebbels dead and burned, and the British press quoting "The day is ours, the bloody dog is dead"'.[9] Mann's account was published (in German) in 1949, but contemporary accounts provide back-up—for example, a short paragraph from the *New York Times* of 2 May 1945: 'In its first comment on the announcement of Hitler's death, the British radio started off: "The day is ours, the bloody dog is dead." That, from the last scene of Shakespeare's "King Richard III", is as good for a first comment on Hitler's death.' It seems likely that this particular quotation will follow the descending arc indicated by the Ngram chart, but nevertheless this particular example of usage, noticed and recorded by a famous German writer, gives it a lasting historical significance (although we may wonder whether even in similar circumstances it would be found acceptable to today's sensibilities).

Out of Context

Established quotations may be brought afresh to public attention in other ways. In 2013, it was announced that Jane Austen was to appear on the new ten-pound note, with the quotation: 'I declare after all there is no enjoyment like reading!' (see Figure 13). In the subsequent news coverage, it was pointed out with some vigour

Figure 13. New British £10 note with a portrait of Jane Austen and the quotation 'I declare after all there is no enjoyment like reading!'

that this was actually the insincere protestation of Miss Bingley. In the scene described in *Pride and Prejudice*, Miss Bingley has chosen her book solely because it is the second volume to the one Mr Darcy is reading. Failing to use it to attract his attention, she is soon 'quite exhausted by the attempt to be amused by her own book'. It is at this point, having endorsed the delight of reading as a pastime ('I declare after all there is no enjoyment like reading! How much sooner one tires of any thing than of a book!'), she yawns, throws the book aside, and begins a conversation about the ball to be given by her brother. Loss of context also completely loses Jane Austen's sense of irony. The literary scholar and journalist John Mullan, writing in the *Guardian* of 25 July 2013, wondered whether the Bank of England governor, Mark Carney, had actually read *Pride and Prejudice*. He evoked the picture of a Bank of England employee asked to find 'the telling Austen quotation. Something about reading perhaps?' The resultant 'quick text search in *Pride and Prejudice* turns up just the thing: "I declare after all there is no enjoyment like reading!"' Unfortunately, the discovery was not accompanied by awareness of the context. However, the news story did ensure that, at least for a time, this would be a very well-known Austen quotation. (A search online establishes that it is also well established on tote bags, mugs, and wall stickers.) And almost certainly it has taken on some separate life: in August 2015, a press release from the *WTNH Connecticut News*, encouraging readers to 'Celebrate National Book Lovers Day with a good read', used the quotation in support: 'As famous novelist Jane Austen once wrote "I declare after all there is no enjoyment like reading! How much sooner one tires of anything than of a book!"'[10] It could in fact be simplistic to put too much weight on the immediate context. Miss Bingley's pretentiousness is set up to be disapproved of by the reader, but her personal insincerity does not mean that Austen herself would not have endorsed the view she gives.

Cultural Significance

Quotations can come to public attention through public art. In January 2016, the BBC broadcast an interview with Niall Macgregor, the outgoing Director of the British Museum, speaking of his successor, the German art historian and museum director Hartwig Fischer. In the course of the interview, Dr Macgregor commented that Hartwig Fischer had known the quotation from Tennyson, 'And let thy feet millenniums hence be built on knowledge', which is inscribed on the floor of the Great Court (see Figure 14). The interviewer queried whether the quotation as it appeared were not incomplete. Niall Macgregor agreed, saying that Dr Fischer had completed it and slightly amplified the meaning. 'It shows the depth of engagement with British culture. It also shows an engagement with ideas at a very deep level and ideas in a public space.'

The question of how the Tennyson quotation might be considered 'incomplete' is worth touching on briefly. As given in the floor of the Great Court, it appears an entirely positive message, appropriately endorsing the pursuit of learning. However, set in context, it is taken from a much less affirmative poem. 'The Two Voices', first published in 1842, was originally written shortly after the death of Arthur Hallam, a time of great unhappiness for Tennyson. The longer passage from which the words here are taken runs:

> 'The highest-mounted mind,' he said
> 'Still sees the sacred morning spread
> The silent summit overhead.

Figure 14. Tennyson quotation on the floor of the Great Court of the British Museum.

'Will thirty seasons render plain
Those lonely lights that still remain,
Just breaking over land and main?

'Or make that morn, from his cold crown
And crystal silence creeping down,
Flood with full daylight glebe and town?

'Forerun thy peers, thy time, and let
Thy feet, millenniums hence, be set
In midst of knowledge, dream'd not yet.' [11]

The poet's son Hallam Tennyson, in his memoir of his father, reported in a footnote: 'My father told me, "When I wrote 'The Two Voices' I was so utterly miserable, a burden to myself and to my family, that I said, 'Is life worth anything?' and now that I am old, I fear that I shall only live a year or two, for I have work still to do."' He had also quoted from the literary editor and biographer James Spedding, writing in the *Edinburgh Review* of April 1843: 'In "The Two Voices" we have a history of the agitations, the suggestions and counter-suggestions of a mind sunk in hopeless despondency.'[12] Knowledge of this wider background is undoubtedly of interest, but does not compromise the separate identity of the quotation as now seen (and walked over) daily by visitors to the Great Court. Quotations are a significant way in which ideas in a public space can be evoked and considered, although some attributions, and out-of-context extractions, have been less acceptable.[13]

Sayings from Literature

Public art has given this Tennyson quotation a higher profile, but it would not necessarily be described as widely known. In contrast, some classic writers have coined phrases that now form part of the language, even if they have not yet qualified as defined items in lexical dictionaries. One example here is 'chaos and old night', from the reference in the first book of Milton's *Paradise Lost* (1667) to the shout that 'tore hell's concave, and beyond Frighted the realm of Chaos and Old Night'.[14]

In 2011, cities in America were confronted by the effects of the 'Occupy Wall Street' campaign against perceived social inequality. A significant protest began in Zuccotti Park, New York, on 17 September 2011. The movement spread, and in November *The Atlantic* reported on the phenomenon under the heading 'Occupy Wall Street and the Return of Law and Order Politics'. Considering reactions, James Poulos wrote: 'In neoconservatism, the disgust familiar to the grassroots conservative fused with the alarm of the intellectual who agreed after all with Russell Kirk that order was foundational, and "the permanent things more pleasing than Chaos and Old Night".'[15] The reference was to the 'Ten Conservative Principles' formulated by the conservative political theorist and writer Russell Kirk (1918–94) and his assertion that, 'in essence, the conservative person is simply one who finds the permanent things more pleasing than Chaos and Old Night'.[16] I find this a really interesting usage. Kirk clearly expects 'chaos and old night' as a term for fundamental disorder to be fully intelligible: the words are being used as a phrase that might be found in a lexical dictionary. Arguably, too, Milton's name has no particular resonance in this context. 'Chaos and old night', however, appears as an idiom without a Miltonic echo.

Productive Passages

A number of literary phrases, once established, demonstrate a capacity for altered wording to a degree that the modification may be regularly used. To take one example from the *Oxford Dictionary of Quotations*, these lines from Pope's character of Addison in the 'Epistle to Dr Arbuthnot' (1735) have been highly productive in terms of language usage.

> Damn with faint praise, assent with civil leer
> And without sneering, teach the rest to sneer.
> Willing to wound, and yet afraid to strike,
> Just hint a fault, and hesitate dislike.[17]

'To damn with faint praise and variants' was added to the OED as a draft lexical item in March 2006.[18] Its usage evidence is strong; recently it appeared in a *Washington Post* column on General Mattis as candidate for Defense Secretary in the incoming administration. Giving the view that the former general was likely to be 'the most impressive individual in the administration', the columnist added the parenthetic disclaimer, 'we don't mean to damn with faint praise'.[19]

'Willing to wound, and yet afraid to strike', unlike 'damn with faint praise', does not appear as a lexical item in the OED, but it is possible to point to a similar level of contemporary evidence, and a respectable history of usage. In January 2017, the columnist Peter Hitchens, castigating the BBC for what he saw as a fictionalized and highly pejorative representation of the campaigner Mary Whitehouse (1910–2001), wrote: 'Of course, the makers of Endeavour didn't dare call this character "Mary Whitehouse". They were willing to wound but afraid to strike.'[20] A decade before, the phrase was frequently used in accounts of the often-fraught relationship between Tony Blair and his eventual successor as prime minister, Gordon Brown. 'Many of the negative impressions of the Chancellor stem from his apparent readiness to plot against Tony Blair. He has come across as willing to wound but afraid to strike.'[21]

This particular quotation has a long usage history. In October 1820, when George IV attempted to divorce his popular wife Caroline of Brunswick, the House of Lords was debating (with some acrimony) a Bill of Pains and Penalties against Her Majesty. One speaker objected to proposed procedure by quoting the key couplet:

> How could they vote the preamble of the bill proved, and then resort to a new measure of a different form? Such conduct would be a gross insult to the unfortunate woman against whom the bill was directed. That, indeed, would show that their lordships were 'willing to wound, and yet afraid to strike'—'Just hint a fault, and hesitate dislike.'[22]

In Henry James's novel *The Portrait of a Lady* (1881) the following exchange occurs between Isabel Archer and her cousin Ralph:

> 'You're beating about the bush, Ralph. You wish to say you don't like Mr Osmond, and yet you're afraid.'
> '"Willing to wound and yet afraid to strike"? I'm willing to wound *him*, yes—but not to wound you. I'm afraid of you, not of him. If you marry him it won't be a fortunate way for me to have spoken.'[23]

In this exchange, Ralph evidently expects Isabel to understand his allusion. He then extends and alters the original meaning, by asserting his readiness to wound one person, but not in the process to hurt another. His use of Pope's phrase, with its pejorative context, also tacitly acknowledges the criticism she makes of his behaviour.

The more established a quotation becomes in the language, the more likely it is to be used allusively, and perhaps to have some of the words varied. A *New York Times* column of February 1931, on what it called 'Britain's tangle of politics', looked at voting patterns in the House of Commons and concluded: 'Many members are willing to strike but afraid to wound.' In 1960, the literary scholar C. S. Lewis published *Studies in Words*, in which he considered the development of various items of vocabulary. At one point, he looked at the way in which the free use of strongly pejorative terms tended to weaken the impact of those terms. He wrote: 'In the field of language ... hatred cuts its own throat, and those who are too "willing to wound" become thereby impotent to strike ... as words become exclusively emotional they cease to be words and therefore of course cease to perform any strictly linguistic function.'[24] Over thirty years later, looking back at his childhood, the playwright John Osborne characterized a determined friend as being 'not so much willing to wound as unafraid to strike'.[25] With the possibility of variation there has also been a weakening of the sense. Pope's original characterization of Addison precisely evoked a malice held back by timidity. Osborne's modified version suggests a more general lack of resolution, in which the concern is that the blow struck may not be a final one.

Forgotten Names?

Shakespeare, Milton, and Pope are all significant authors whose names (and works) resonate today. However, in considering the 'classical' canon, it is appropriate to look at names that were once highly resonant, but that no longer carry their original associations.

One significant example here is Jean-Paul-François de Gondi, Cardinal de Retz (1613–79), a noted power-broker in seventeenth-century France. He is still quoted, but not necessarily in a way that requires knowledge of his history or political personality. Googling 'de Retz' and 'quotations' is likely to bring up a number of (authentic) sayings that are presented without context. Sites such as *ThinkExist* and *The Quotations Page* carry genuine de Retz quotations such as 'a man who doesn't trust himself can never really trust anyone else' and 'it is even more damaging for a minister to say foolish things than to do them'.[26] They are presented as sayings that are still valid, but that, if quoted today, are unlikely to be accompanied by 'as de Retz says' or a similar parenthesis. The cardinal, once notable, is not in the twenty-first century a significant figure.

Perhaps most famously, one of his sayings was used as an epigraph to an iconic book by the photographer Henri Cartier-Bresson (1908–2004). De Retz had written in his memoirs that 'there is nothing in the world which does not have its decisive moment'.[27] Cartier-Bresson utilized this as the epigraph to his 1952 book *Image à la sauvette* (referring to an image taken 'on the run' or without authorization), which was then published in English as *The Decisive Moment*.[28] The quotation thus carries considerable weight, but does not reflect with any significance the perceived character of de Retz. We can see the difference if we look at eighteenth- and nineteenth-century instances of sources in which de Retz was quoted.

Admired in the eighteenth and nineteenth centuries, his memoirs were read (and maxims collected) by the politician and diplomat Lord Chesterfield (1694–1773) and James Madison (1751–1836), Founding Father and fourth president of the United States. Chesterfield (1694–1773) saw de Retz as a figure who repaid study. As he wrote in 1748, recommending the *Memoirs* to his son:

The Memoirs of the Cardinal de Retz will both entertain and instruct you: they relate to a very interesting period of the French history, the ministry of Cardinal Mazarin, during the minority of Lewis XIV. The characters of all the considerable people of that time are drawn, in a short, strong, and masterly manner; and the political reflections, which are most of them printed in italics, are the justest that ever I met with: they are not the laboured reflections of a systematical closet politician, who, without the least experience, sits at home and writes maxims; but they are the reflections which a great and able man formed from long experience and practice in great business. They are true conclusions, drawn from facts, not from speculation.[29]

Chesterfield's characterization of the cardinal as a 'great and able man' is somewhat qualified elsewhere. He extracted a list (in French) of sixty-seven of these maxims, and they were published (with a translation) in his posthumous *Miscellaneous Pieces*.[30] His accompanying notes about the cardinal were a little less enthusiastic. He was a 'man of parts' but 'not truly a great man'. Some years later in the American colonies, the youthful James Madison compiled an 'Abstract from the Memoirs of the Cardinal de Retz' in his Commonplace Book.[31] Like Chesterfield, he copied out maxims that presumably appealed to him.

Cited by David Hume (1711–76) and Adam Smith (1723–90), de Retz was a known figure up to the eighteenth century as a type of powerful and cunning politician. Hume references him in *A Treatise of Human Nature*:

From the same principles we may account for those observations of the Cardinal De Retz, that *there are many things in which the world wishes to be deceiv'd*; and *that it more easily excuses a person in acting than in talking contrary to the decorum of his profession and character.*[32]

Smith quotes him more than once in *The Theory of Moral Sentiments* (1759) and adds some characterization. He is linked with Cardinal Richelieu as a statesman whose projects had been 'very daring and extensive, though altogether devoid of justice'. At another point, Smith adds to his name the parenthetic comment, 'a man not over-credulous in the virtue of other people'. One apparent 'quotation' (for which a direct original has not been traced) is a statement about the limitations of political leadership: 'The head of a party, the Cardinal de Retz observes, may do what he pleases; as long as he retains the confidence of his own friends, he can never do wrong; a maxim of which his Eminence had himself, upon several occasions, an opportunity of experiencing the truth.'[33] It seems likely that this is in fact a paraphrase of de Retz's thought rather than intended as a direct quotation. The editors of the Glasgow edition of Smith's *Works* call the attribution a mistake, but add in a note to this passage that 'he did make several other observations (some not altogether unlike this one, others tending to contradict it) about parties and their heads'.

De Retz's reflections on political leadership found an echo across the Atlantic some years later, in a biographical account of governors of the State of New York. The author, however, truncated de Retz's supposed assertion, thus changing the emphasis. He wrote: '"The head of a party", said Cardinal De Retz, "can do what he pleases". However true this may be in monarchical governments, it is the exception, rather than the rule, in a republic. We have had but one Washington, and but one Jackson.'[34] Awareness of de Retz was alive in the nineteenth century, as in Isaac D'Israeli's *The Literary Character* (1818).[35] In it D'Israeli described the cardinal as 'one of those pretended patriots without a single of those virtues for which he was the clamorous advocate of faction'.

And while in a later edition he described the cardinal as 'this great genius', his summing up of de Retz was otherwise unchanged.[36]

Isaac's knowledge of the cardinal seems to have been passed on to his son. In his 1966 biography of Benjamin Disraeli, Robert Blake describes an exchange between the younger Disraeli and the politician and philanthropist Lord Rowton (1838–1903). Blake repeats what Lord Rowton had recorded in the 1870s of Disraeli's comment on his father's failure to grasp the details of his son's political rise, and the fall of Robert Peel, whom he thought 'a good sort of man, and the only one popular in the country'. As Rowton understood it:

> He never realized that D., not approving of Peel's policy, saw the situation, and had the boldness to make the onslaught alone, confident in the truth of the Cardinal de Retz's maxim, 'Il n'y a rien dans le monde qui n'ait son moment decisive: et le chef d'œuvre de la bonne conduit est de connoitre et de prendre ce moment' (D. has just pointed out this passage to me).[37]

The words that struck Disraeli were those on which Cartier-Bresson was to fasten in 1952.

Minor Survivals

Quotations considered in this chapter have typically originated with famous names, most of which are resonant today. The usage history of quotations ascribed to figures previously discussed has both longevity and a degree of depth. It is possible, however, to find instances of quotations where a fairly long usage history can be traced for a comparatively minor item that has never spread beyond a few people. A column in *The Times* of October 1961 opened up a picture of the 'quotation life' of a particular item in its account of a researcher attempting to verify a quotation for use in the House of Commons by Winston Churchill.[38] The lines sought turned out to come from a once-popular but by then largely forgotten poet, William Watson (1858–1935). According to the *Oxford Dictionary of National Biography*, Watson had been spoken of as a possible poet laureate when Tennyson died in 1892. In 1902 he had published a well-received poem, *Ode on the Coronation of King Edward VII*, which would have fitted this profile. However, as well as being 'out of step with modernist trends in literature', Watson was highly critical of government policy as manifested in Britain's actions in the South African War. In 1904 he published *For England: Verses Written in Estrangement*. This collection included his poem 'The True Imperialism', with the lines:

> Is there no room for victories here?
> No field for deeds of shame?[39]

Churchill (who would not have been in sympathy with Watson's anti-imperialist stance) knew of them as a favourite quotation of the liberal politician Charles Masterman and had clearly retained them in his mind since Masterman's death in 1927.[40] Watson's lines were also demonstrably known to Leslie Hale (1902–85), a Labour politician who sat for Oldham between 1945 and 1968, but whose political career had begun when he contested the South Nottingham constituency for the Liberal Party in 1929. He quoted them in the House of Commons in 1950, coincidentally shortly prior to Churchill's own employment of the lines, and then again in the House of Lords in 1973. On that occasion, the then Lord Hale (he had been ennobled in 1972) had put forward a motion on the need for increased Commonwealth consultation, something that did not find favour with Lord Thurlow. Opposing the motion, he spoke of 'those who indulge in incantations of the Commonwealth as a mysterious force that works by sacramental magic'. Lord Hale, returning hurriedly to the Chamber as soon as he realized that the debate had been resumed, came in 'in the middle of a sentence about incantations' and was unsure whether the reference was to his own allusions or those made in other speeches. 'I was not quite sure ... whether he was against "Onward, Christian Soldiers, Marching as to war", or whether he was against William Watson the Lancashire poet who said: "Is there no room for victories here, no field for deeds of fame."'[41] He proceeded to quote this verse from 'The True Imperialism' in its entirety, down to 'And build within the mind of man the Empire that abides'.

It appeared, then, that Watson's lines had a certain currency in Liberal circles from the first part of the twentieth century, something that is underscored by a very early usage, of 1905. In January of that year, Sir Henry Campbell-Bannerman, Leader of the Liberal Party and MP for Stirling Burghs, was speaking in Stirling. As reported in the *Manchester Guardian* of 18 January, he concluded his speech with the peroration:

> More and more vain is your science, vain your art, your triumphs, and your glories—vain to feed the hunger of their heart and forming of their brain. Your savage deserts howling near your wastes of ignorance, vice, and shame—is there no room for victories here, no field for deeds of fame?[42]

Quoting the rest of Watson's verse in full, he apparently 'resumed his feet among loud and prolonged cheers, after having spoken for one hour and eleven minutes'.

It is probably not surprising that William Watson's stance on the role of the British in the South African War recommended him warmly to Liberal and radical opinion. The line can effectively be traced from Campbell-Bannerman and Masterman to their younger contemporary and one-time fellow Liberal Winston Churchill and then to Leslie Hale.

Following Hale's second citation of Watson's lines, I have not been able to find further evidence of usage in British political discourse—presumably because the nature of 'imperialism' was no longer seen as a central national question. It is possible, however, to say from the evidence that, over a period of nearly seventy years, 'no room for victories' had an initial currency in Liberal and radical circles, which was extended through the political lifetimes of two or three politicians—an instance of the part that can be played by a personal vocabulary of quotations.

CHAPTER 5

HIDDEN MEANINGS AND SPECIAL LINKS

Some quotations have an association that allows them to operate a kind of coded reference. The surface meaning makes perfect sense, but knowledge of the origin of the quotation adds a special context to those who are aware of it. A striking example was provided in March 2017, in the aftermath of the terrorist attack on Westminster Bridge in London, which culminated inside the precincts of the Houses of Parliament. Writing in the London *Times* on the proper response by a democracy to this kind of outrage, the journalist Philip Collins concluded his column: 'Conceptually and intellectually the search for utopia is over and liberal democracy is the last world. These moments of terror show us that earth has not anything to show more fair.' What he writes makes perfect literal sense, but is given extra force by the final words. These are an allusion to the opening lines of Wordsworth's 1807 sonnet 'Composed upon Westminster Bridge':

> Earth has not anything to show more fair:[1]
> Dull would he be of soul who could pass by
> A sight so touching in its majesty.

The sonnet's evocation of the calm beauty evoked by the morning view of Westminster is a striking contrast to the violent context of a terrorist onslaught.

Signalling Contexts

On 2 February 2016, the *Dundalk Democrat* carried the report that a local antique shop, Euro Antiques and Collectables, had put on a display of 1916 memorabilia. Products in the shop now included 'Ireland Unfree Shall Never Be at Peace'.[2] In the centenary year of the Easter Rising, the plaques illuminated one of the most evocative quotations of nationalist Ireland (see Figure 15). The words come from the oration by Patrick Pearse (in 1916, one of the executed leaders of the Easter Rising) over the grave of the Fenian Jeremiah O'Donovan Rossa. O'Donovan Rossa had died in America, and his body was brought back for burial in Ireland. The closing words of Pearse's speech at the graveside were to become iconic: 'The fools, the fools, the fools!—they have left us our Fenian dead, and

Figure 15. Graffito showing the sentence in Patrick Pearse's oration from which the slogan 'Ireland unfree shall never be at peace' is taken.

while Ireland holds these graves, Ireland unfree shall never be at peace.'[3]

For anyone familiar with Irish Republican history, the words are indelibly associated with a key figure of the Republican pantheon. Their importance was underlined in 1926, when the speech from which the words come was incorporated by Sean O'Casey in *The Plough and the Stars*. The play was first staged at the Abbey Theatre in February of that year, and nationalist rioters who objected to the view given of the Easter Rising staged a protest. Subsequently, the *Irish Times* of 2 March carried an account of a lecture given under the auspices of the University Republican Club by Mrs Sheehy-Skeffington. The subject was *The Plough and the Stars*, 'the production of which recently at the Abbey Theatre provoked "scenes" in the body of the theatre'. The lecturer, claiming the right of an audience to assert disapproval by 'hissing or booing', had expressed the view that this was 'not a typical picture of the men of 1916' and was without 'a gleam of heroism'. Sean O'Casey, proposing a vote of thanks to the speaker, used his right of reply to defend the play. He was trying to write not about heroes, but about 'the life and the people' that he knew. (It seems likely that his audience was generally unpersuaded: the seconder to the vote of thanks is recorded as saying that *The Plough and the Stars* was 'an anti-Pearse play'.)

However, it would also be possible for the words to be understood on a surface level only, as the direct assertion of a current political position, without any awareness of its historical context. A photograph of Queen Elizabeth II in Boston Massachusetts in July 1976 shows her walking past a number of demonstrators. One holds up a placard reading 'Ireland unfree shall never be at peace'. Presumably not everyone who saw the picture would have been aware of the origin of the words.

In 2002, a Conservative politician called Theresa May occasioned some indignation among colleagues when she told the Conservative conference of that year, in the aftermath of a general election in which they had once more been defeated: 'You know what some people call us? The nasty party.'[4] The phrase was remembered (and quoted) during the succeeding years of opposition, but it gained new significance when in 2016, in the aftermath of Brexit, Theresa May became prime minister. A cartoon by Peter Brookes, following the death of the actor Gene Wilder in 2016, testified to its memorability. One of Wilder's most famous roles had been that of the hapless Leo Bloom in the Mel Brooks's 1968 film *The Producers*. The accountant Leopold Bloom (Wilder) and the producer Max Bialystock attempt to produce a musical that cannot succeed—*Springtime for Hitler*, the title song of which included the adjuration:

> Don't be stupid, be a smarty
> Come and join the Nazi Party.

Brookes, in a cartoon 'RIP Gene Wilder. Springtime for Brexit' showing Theresa May and her three Brexit ministers marching in Storm Troopers' uniform, added a speech bubble with the reworked lines:

> Don't be stupid, be a smarty
> Come and join the Nasty Party.[5]

It was clearly his assumption that the reference would be understood, and that assumption is strengthened by a teasing reference made by the prime minister herself in her speech to the Conservative conference of October 2016. Surveying the Labour

Party's internal problems, she summarized: 'You know what some people call them? The nasty party.'[6] Clearly it was to be expected that her audience would understand the reference, but it seems equally evident that she and her speech-writers were confident that the soundbite would reach a wider public—which, as subsequent headlines attested, it did.[7]

Hidden Warnings

In December 2015, the American journalist and writer P. J. O'Rourke published a satirical account of American presidential candidates, with particular concentration on those he perceived as likely to be supported by older voters. Part of the column read as follows:

> Enter Ben Carson. Caldron boiling.
> *Eye of Newt (Gingrich), facts of fog,*
> *Hare of brain, tongue of blog …*
> Bernie Sanders is going to and fro in the earth.
> And then there's Trump—Landlord of the Flies.[8]

The first and third references (respectively to the Weird Sisters in Shakespeare's *Macbeth*, and to the title of William Golding's novel *Lord of the Flies*, itself a title for Beelzebub) are likely to be immediately recognizable, but 'going to and fro in the earth' may not strike an immediate chord. In fact, the allusion is also demonic. It was employed very effectively by Thomas Harris in his bestselling *The Silence of the Lambs* (1988), in relation to the terrible Dr Hannibal Lecter. In the relevant scene, Dr Lecter has escaped from custody (with his trademark intelligence and savagery) and has checked into a luxurious hotel. 'The suite seemed enormous to Dr Lecter after his long confinement. He enjoyed going to and fro in his suite and walking up and down in it.'[9] The quoted words make perfect literal sense in terms of Hannibal Lecter's enjoyment of the freedom of his suite after the restrictions of a prison cell, but for someone familiar with traditional biblical usage, the final sentence functions as a code signalling his demonic nature. The reference is to the biblical Book of Job, chapter 1, verse 7: 'And the Lord said unto Satan, whence comest thou? Then Satan answered the Lord, and said, From going to and fro in the earth, and from walking up and down in it.'[10]

The use of a less familiar biblical quote functioning as a coded reference was signalled when, in September 2015, it was announced that the original recordings of three Agatha Christie plays, long thought lost, had been discovered in the BBC Archive. First broadcast between 1948 and 1960, they were issued by BBC Audio as a double CD and as a download. One of the plays was entitled *Butter in a Lordly Dish*. The main character is a successful barrister and, from a conversation between his long-suffering wife and a friend of hers, it becomes clear that he is a philanderer. Returning from securing a conviction, he is soon on his way to an assignation with an attractive lady, who takes him off to her weekend cottage (see Figure 16).

It is not difficult to build up a picture of Luke. He is a highly successful barrister who appears for the prosecution and who is a wholehearted supporter of the death penalty. Julia, his recently met lady friend, questions him about the case of a murderer he prosecuted some years before. She plies him with wine and food, and he is particularly struck by the mountain of butter served with the caviare. It stirs up some kind of unpleasant association, but he cannot quite remember what it is.

Figure 16. Programme announcement of Agatha Christie's play *Butter in a Lordly Dish*.

At this point, it becomes clear that Julia has made some addition to what she has served him. Luke is growing drowsy, but he is awake enough to be surprised when she produces a hammer—and possibly too at this point he makes the necessary connection. In any case (and in a scene of some melodrama) Julia reveals that she is the widow of a man hanged for murder, convicted in one of Luke's successful prosecutions. (The fact that she herself had been the killer rather than her husband seems to have fuelled her anger.) The scene fades out in a sinister fusillade of hammering.

Luke, unfortunately for him, did not decode the symbolism of the lavish dish of butter, but in the 1940s the reference might have been expected to find some echoes. It goes back to a biblical story in the fifth chapter of the Old Testament book of Judges. Sisera, commander of an enemy army, has been routed in battle with Israel. In flight, he seeks refuge in the tent of Jael, wife of Heber. She is apparently hospitable. 'He asked water, and she gave him milk; she brought forth butter in a lordly dish.'[11] However, when (presumably exhausted) he falls asleep, she kills him by driving a nail through his temples.

Agatha Christie no doubt chose her title carefully, possibly with the view that it might awake echoes but not be immediately transparent. Earlier twentieth-century evidence can be adduced both for use of the phrase in the context of the story of Jael's revenge on Sisera, and for less sinister interpretation. It is of interest here to look at an anecdote recounted by John Ruskin in *Praeterita* (1885–9), his unfinished autobiography. He describes attending a Bible study on the story of Jael and Sisera given by his friend F. D. Maurice, Principal of the Working Men's College. Maurice took 'an enlightened modern view' of the propriety of Jael's actions and seems to have been concerned that they might be taken as too literal a model. Having warned his class that 'such dreadful deeds could only have been taken in cold blood in the "Dark Biblical Ages"', he enforced this with the comment that 'no religious and patriotic Englishwoman ought ever to think of imitating Jael by nailing a Prussian's or Russian's skull to the ground—especially after giving him butter in a lordly dish'.[12]

Ruskin would have expected his readers to be familiar with the story, but the weight on the key phrase does emphasize the (apparent) lavish hospitality rather than the ensuing treachery. If we look more widely, it is possible to find instances where the fate of the unfortunate Sisera has been completely detached from the instance of his betrayal. *The American Cyclopedia of Illustrations for Public Speakers*, published in 1911, appears to recommend it as a desirable phrase. 'A kindness or a benefaction dealt in a courteous spirit and in fine chivalry is equally "butter in a lordly dish".'[13]

Coming forward, an exchange in the House of Commons in a debate of 1939 supports this approach. A speaker commented on the rejection by the representative of the opposing party of an amendment to a bill that would have offered him 'wide and considerable powers'.[14] He added: 'We are really bringing him butter on a lordly dish, and, unfortunately for him, he is compelled to resist the offer.' This provoked the response: 'Is that surprising, considering the fate of the gentleman who was offered the lordly dish?' To which he was obliged to confess: 'That fate had escaped my attention.' It was explained to him that 'the poor gentleman had a tent peg—supplied, I suppose, by a Service Department—driven through his head'. His reply—'I can tell the hon. Gentleman at once that that slipped my memory'—asserted firmly his essential familiarity with the story. The House of Commons in 1939 clearly contained members who remembered their Authorized Version, and those who were less well versed in it. The episode also demonstrates that 'butter in a lordly dish' is a quotation that was capable of being used with or without conscious allusion to the original context. In 1940, the *Irish Law Times* used it in a report on one of the edicts of Lord Woolton, the Conservative politician who was the wartime Minister of Food. The comment ran: 'Lord Woolton has brought forth butter in a lordly dish, saying that *bona fide* unsolicited gifts, whether they include rationed foods or not, may be received from abroad by parcel post provided they are addressed to individuals.'[15] 'Butter in a lordly dish' here is used to suggest generosity through association with richness; there is no indication that the gifts referred to might mask enmity. And a debate in the House of Commons from the same period backs up the view that the phrase, while sometimes recognized, was not universally known.

It is valid to ask today whether Christie's title would still provoke unease, and it seems quite likely that the phrase has now to a considerable degree died from sight—not least because modern biblical translations render it very differently. It can be found variously as 'curds in a bowl fit for a chieftain' (New English Bible), 'cream in a beautiful bowl' (Good News Bible), and 'curdled milk' in 'a bowl fit for nobles' (New International Version)—all so different as to be virtually unrecognizable. And, as a more general figure of speech, 'butter in a lordly dish' now has something of an archaic ring.

Special Associations

Individual phrases, without carrying a particular coded reference, may take on an association and context, as exemplified by the history of 'splendid misery'. In itself, as an expression denoting a situation in which outward luxury is accompanied by inner unhappiness and powerlessness, it is transparent in terms of meaning, with no special idiomatic sense. In the language of the twenty-first century, it has a somewhat archaic ring. We would not expect to find it defined in a lexical dictionary, or feel the need to consult a dictionary in order to decode it. However, investigation of its life in the language reveals the attachment of a particular association.[16]

In American usage, 'splendid misery' has a particular association with the perceived burdens of the office of the presidency, as exemplified in November 2016 by a comment on the upcoming presidential election that considered the question of why candidates might run for a position that offered such pressure and such scrutiny: 'This is not a position that brings great wealth. It is a position that really is a very, very hard job. Thomas Jefferson memorably described the presidency as a splendid misery.'[17]

Eight years before, the columnist Maureen O'Dowd had written of Barack Obama's acceptance speech that it was 'stark and simple', and showed that he knew what he would be up against. 'There was a heaviness in his demeanor, as if he already had taken on the isolation and "splendid misery", as Jefferson called it, of the office he'd won only moments before.'[18] The expression 'splendid misery' in this context was used by Thomas Jefferson in a letter of 13 May 1797 to Elbridge Gerry, written after Jefferson had become vice-president. In the letter, Jefferson said: 'The second office of government is honourable and easy, the first is but a splendid misery.'[19] It is quite possible that the phrase was current in political circles at the time, since three days after Jefferson's letter it was employed by the new First Lady, Abigail Adams, of her own situation. 'Mrs [Cotton] Tufts once stiled my situation, splendid misery. She was not far from Truth.'[20] However, it was the association with Jefferson, and the presidency, that was to last. Most obviously, Jefferson's was clearly the more resonant name. It is also worth noting the comparative speeds with which the material reached the public domain. Jefferson's papers, including the letter to Gerry, were published in 1829.[21] The letter in which Abigail Adams used the phrase, by contrast, seems not to have been collected in a published volume of her letters until the twentieth century.

'Splendid misery' as a phrase was not coined by Jefferson. A seventeenth-century example exists, in a comment by the clergyman John Dunton (1628–76) on grand titles likely to be used by the Ottoman ruler Suleiman the Magnificent. Dunton thought poorly of such honorifics as 'Emperor of Trebizond and Constantinople' and 'Lord of the World', describing them as 'truely splendid misery' and 'ashes and nothing'.[22] In the eighteenth century, the British poet Edward Young employed it to convey a situation of unhappiness in the midst of riches and luxury:

> Can wealth give happiness? Look round, and see
> What gay distress! What splendid misery![23]

This arguably became a well-known usage, since Young's lines can be found in some of the main nineteenth-century dictionaries of quotations, such as H. G. Bohn's *A Dictionary of Quotations from the English and American Poets* (1883) and Hoyt and Ward's *A Cyclopaedia of Practical Quotations* (1882).

Throughout the eighteenth and nineteenth centuries, 'splendid misery' recurs in neutral and literal uses very close to cliché. It figured in a British copyright case of 1881, when another writer objected to the popular novelist Mary Elizabeth Braddon's employing it as a title on the grounds that this would infringe his own copyright. Mrs Braddon was a well-known 'sensation' novelist, author of the extremely successful *Lady Audley's Secret* (1862); she also lived with her publisher John Maxwell as his wife, a circumstance that gave rise to scandal.[24] A case involving one of her books (the immediate successor to *Lady Audley's Secret*, whose bigamous and murderous heroine had shocked Mrs Braddon's fellow author Mrs Oliphant) was likely to be of public interest.

The case ultimately went to the Court of Appeal, which came down firmly against the possibility of anyone holding copyright in such a phrase. The Master of the Rolls questioned whether there could 'be copyright at all in these words', and answered his own question: 'I think not.' He was supported by his fellow judge Sir Robert Lush, who is quoted as saying:

> How can it be said that there is anything original in these two words? I suppose there is hardly a person who has grown up to maturity in this country who has not read them hundreds of times, and heard them spoken hundreds of times. To my mind it is a hackneyed phrase.[25]

He concluded that there was no originality in the title, or anything that indicated intellectual effort. 'It is merely the taking up a phrase which had been in public use before, and had become public property.' For the Appeal judges, and probably the wider British public, 'splendid misery' was little more than a cliché, appropriate enough for the world of the sensation novel, but with no more serious connotation. They regarded the phrase as one that would be widely familiar, but that for this reason could not possibly be copyrighted. (Certainly neither of them seems to have been aware of any link to the American Founding Fathers[26] and the burdens of presidential office.) The result of their deliberations was to enshrine the principle of British copyright law that there 'there can in general be no copyright in the title or name of a book', but it is unlikely today that the actual phrase would evoke memories of the case.

It was not a complete win for Mrs Braddon, since, while the case was proceeding, her wished-for title of *Splendid Misery* could not be used as it stood. When the book appeared in 1880, under a rather longer title, she provided a preliminary 'Explanation', which included the following:

> As matters now stand, the Author feels constrained to give prominence to the name of her heroine in the title of her book, which she according sends forth as THE STORY OF BARBARA; HER SPLENDID MISERY, and HER GILDED CAGE, in the belief that no one can take exception either to a mere Christian name, when used in the title of a novel, or to the trebly distinctive title now given to a book that was written to amuse the public, and not to exercise the copyright lawyers.[27]

In the twentieth century, neutral uses of 'splendid misery' gradually died out, presumably because the expression had become increasingly archaic. It would probably be unsafe to say that anything that fits into the discourse of purple prose could not be found at all, but certainly the majority of instances that do occur are found in association with the topic of the American presidency, and/or Thomas Jefferson. *Time* magazine of July 1959 considered the pressures on Dwight Eisenhower,[28] under the heading 'The Presidency: Splendid Misery', pointing out that, in his first year of office, the first president, George Washington, had approved only twenty-seven laws, and had done little towards budget-making other than by signing a short document prepared by Congress. 'Thomas Jefferson, whose chores were not much heavier, called the presidency "splendid misery".' By contrast, as *Time* pointed out, President Eisenhower in a typical year might sign 750 bills, and take responsibility for a budget filling over 1,100 small-print pages. Ten years later, the *Chicago Tribune* used the expression in connection with another president and the difficulties of office. As their columnist wrote: 'In two months in the While House, President Nixon has learned what a splendid misery the leadership of the nation can be.'[29]

In the second half of the twentieth century, the expression was well known enough to be used in book titles. For example, a 1960 book by Jack Bell had the title *The Splendid Misery; The Story of the Presidency and Power Politics at Close Range*. In 1993, Richard H. Hunt published *A Splendid Misery: Challenges of Thomas Jefferson's Presidency*. In the twenty-first century, it is less common, but examples do still occur, as on the radio programme *Talk of the Nation*, broadcast 14 September 2009. The background was an incident of a few days before, when President Obama's address to a joint session of Congress on healthcare reform was interrupted by Congressman Joe Wilson's shouted comment: 'You lie!' The affair was discussed on *Talk of the Nation*, hosted by Neil Conan, under the heading 'Where's the Line between Dissent and Disrespect?' One of the guests on the programme was the historian Robert Dallek, and he reached back to Jefferson's words as a summary of the kind of critical attack that a president might expect. Neil Conan, noting that former presidents such as Lincoln had been subjected to verbal 'vitriol', commented: 'Outside of the halls of Congress, just about anything goes, right?' Dallek responded: 'Yeah, exactly. In fact, Thomas Jefferson described the presidency as a splendid misery because of all this kind of criticism, the constant drumbeat of attacks.'

'Splendid misery', then, is a phrase that historically has two quite separate resonances, although it remains transparent in terms of its essential meaning. In American usage, it now has an ineradicable link with the perceived burdens of the presidency, as described by Thomas Jefferson (whose name is almost certain to be mentioned when the expression is used). In British English, it is part of legal history in being linked with a landmark copyright case. In itself, however, it is probably now not used sufficiently to justify the 1881 description of 'hackneyed'. If found in general use, it would be likely to be thought of as a somewhat archaic expression, with a similar meaning to the figurative 'bird in a gilded cage', but with distinctly less popularity. Mrs Braddon's difficulties with her chosen title would find few memories today. Nevertheless, it is a phrase whose surface lack of interest conceals a history with links to two distinct sets of contextual association.

CHAPTER 6

QUOTATIONS ON THE MOVE

The *Oxford English Dictionary* entry for 'misquotation' (updated in 2002) lays considerable emphasis on inaccuracy. The two-part definition reads:

a. An incorrect or inaccurate quotation.
b. Inaccuracy in quoting.

The balance of the illustrative quotations supports this emphasis, beginning with the earliest, from 1612, which refers to 'Infinite faults … as misquotations, mistaking of sillables, misplacing half lines, coining of strange and neuer head of words'. (The author, the dramatist and poet Thomas Heywood, was lamenting the 'negligence of the printer' of his 1609 poem *Troia Britanica*.[1]) Another quotation, from three centuries later, comes from Charles Dickens in *Sketches by Boz* (1836). Dickens is writing of wealthy Uncle Tom, who is such a devotee of Shakespeare that he knows the principal plays by heart. 'The result of this parrot-like accomplishment was, that he was not only perpetually quoting himself, but that he could never sit by, and hear a misquotation from the "Swan of Avon" without setting the unfortunate delinquent right.'[2] While the desire for accuracy is to be applauded, it is difficult to feel great enthusiasm for Uncle Tom, especially where what is in question might be no more than a verbal slip or minor alteration in conversation. The poet and classicist A. E. Housman, known for his textual rigour, was in one instance at least less severe. He had been visited by the American defence attorney Clarence Darrow, who in 1924 had famously come out of retirement to defend the young killers Leopold and Loeb. He had only a short time in England, but was determined to visit Housman, whose poetry he had often used 'to rescue his clients from the electric chair'. Darrow's powerful plea for mitigation on behalf of Leopold and Loeb (through which the death sentence had been avoided) included quoting the whole of Housman's poem 'The Culprit' from *Last Poems*, in which a young man faces death by hanging. He thought Leopold and Loeb owed their escape at least partly to Housman. Writing ruefully to his brother, Housman reported that Darrow had given him a copy of the speech 'in which, sure enough, two of my pieces are misquoted'.[3] There is, however, no indication that he had emulated Uncle Tom and put Darrow right.

Reflecting on this prompts the question, is there no more to misquotation than inaccuracy and error? I would like to suggest that there is, something that is signalled in the *OED*'s most recent illustrative citation for 'misquotation', provided by the British psychoanalyst and writer Marion Milner (1900–98). This runs: 'Misquotations are often as meaningful as the quotations themselves.' Looking at the fuller passage from which the words come, we find that Milner is describing the process of revising diary 'jottings' that she had made over past years. She was interested particularly in 'bits of the Bible', which she had deliberately refrained from looking up to check the wording. Partly, she wanted to see how much of her early religious education had survived, but, more importantly, she recognized misquotation as a potentially creative process. It is this area that I intend to consider here. I suggest that evidence shows that once quotations establish themselves in the language they may become as subject to language change, and as productive, as any fixed phrase or other lexical item.[4] In this chapter, I shall look at some examples of quotations that are 'on the move', establishing an alternative form that may become part of the public vocabulary.

Fallible Memory

Typically, we quote what we remember, but this can be shifting ground. An anecdote about Leonard and Virginia Woolf makes the point. In his *Autobiography* (1967) the philosopher Bertrand Russell attributed to the socialist and historian Sidney Webb the summary 'marriage is the waste-paper basket of the emotions'. There are a number of sources that attribute the comment to Sidney's wife Beatrice, qualified by the words 'we always say'. However, the source that demonstrates possible complexities to the full is Leonard Woolf's autobiography *Beginning Again* (1964). Leonard describes a visit made by the Webbs to the Woolfs in 1918. They went out for an evening walk, and at one point Sidney was walking with Leonard at some distance from their wives. Looking back, Sidney told Leonard that he knew what Beatrice Webb was saying to Virginia. 'She is saying that marriage is the waste paper basket of the emotions.'[5] Later that evening, Virginia confirmed these words, as accompanied by the parenthetic 'we always say.' So far so good, but Leonard's account included a footnote that offers a perfect picture of the difficulties inherent in verification.

He noted as a 'curious fact' that the account of the conversation in Virginia's diary reported Beatrice as saying that 'marriage was necessary as a waste pipe for emotion'. He reflected on the difficulty of being certain 'of any accuracy' in recorded conversations, although he was sure that Sidney had used the words he had reported. He was slightly less confident ('almost certain') that Virginia had agreed with him that that was what Beatrice had said to her. However, he admitted ruefully that it was impossible to be sure. 'Virginia was never an accurate recorder of what people said.' Her diary was written three days after the events, and it was 'possible, if not probable', that 'she dashed down (inaccurately) waste pipe'. It was, he concluded, impossible to know.

The existence of a written source does not always solve the problem.

We edit as we remember, often reducing a longer original to a pithier summary. In August 2014, Gerrie Nel, prosecutor in the trial of Oscar Pistorius, was reported as citing John Mortimer's 'Rumpole of the Bailey' as saying that 'a criminal trial is a very blunt instrument for digging out the truth'. The passage from which this comes is rather longer. Rumpole, considering a client, reflects: 'I didn't like to tell her that a criminal trial, before a judge, who comes armed with his own prejudices, and a jury, whose attention frequently wanders, may be a pretty blunt instrument for prising out the truth.'[6] Nel, in other words, was taking the gist of Rumpole's reflection, trimming away the parenthetic comments on the respective tendencies of juries and judges. The pithier version is then further strengthened by substituting 'very blunt' for 'pretty blunt'. It would be harsh, however, to suggest that Rumpole's essential meaning has been distorted or obscured, so we may wonder to what degree this should be classed as a misquotation.

Allusive Uses

Reworking may be designed to echo and contrast with a significant original. The journalist Nick Cohen, in a 2011 column on western misunderstanding of Middle Eastern politics, used a quotation from Auden to drive home his point:

> In his Epitaph on a Tyrant, Auden wrote:
>
> *'When he laughed, respectable senators burst with laughter*
> *And when he cried, the little children died in the streets.'*
>
> Europe's amnesia about how tyranny operated in our continent explains why the Libyan revolution is embarrassing a rich collection of dupes and scoundrels who were willing to laugh along with Gaddafi.[7]

Auden's 'Epitaph on a Tyrant', of which these are the concluding words, was published in 1940. Its evocation of a ruthless dictator would have been given extra force by its echoing of a famous nineteenth-century encomium of a very different kind of ruler. The American historian John Lothrop Motley (1814–77) had written of the seventeenth-century Protestant hero William of Orange, 'the Silent', founding father of the Dutch state, 'As long as he lived, he was the guiding-star of a brave nation, and when he died the little children cried in the streets'.[8]

Edmund Burke has become a favourite authority to cite in right-wing thought, both in Britain and in America.[9] Theresa May referenced him at her first party conference as Conservative leader and prime minister, telling her audience that, 'from Edmund Burke onwards, Conservatives have always understood that if you want to preserve something important, you need to be prepared to reform it'.[10] It looks as though this is a reflection of a summary of Burke's views that has come through a particular source. In Chapter 4, considering references to 'chaos and old night', I looked at a reference by the right-wing political theorist Russell Kirk.[11] Under his 'Ten Conservative Principles', Kirk noted in a parenthetic comment that 'Conservatives know, with Burke, that healthy "change is the means of our preservation"'. A little investigation demonstrates that, from the 1980s on, this 'quotation' appears quite frequently—often in studies on the New Right, or from that area of thought, and usually referenced to Burke. However, before that the earliest instance found is from 1964.[12] Prior to that, there are no instances found. What seems likely is that 'change is the means of our preservation' originates in a genuine quotation that linked change and conservation. In May 2016, considering the recent local elections, the *Times* leader considered prospects for the Conservative government, and invoked Burke's name, calling him 'the wandering Whig who became an improbable lodestar of modern Tory thought'. The leader quoted from a letter of Burke's written 'to a colleague' (the Irish politician Sir Hercules Langrishe) in which he said: 'We must all obey the great law of change. It is the most powerful law of nature, and the means perhaps of its conservation.'[13] It was not the only time when Burke associated change and conservation. He did so in *Reflections on the Revolution in France* (1791): 'A state without the means of some change is without the means of its conservation.'[14] The *Times* leader shows that the thought has resonance today—however, there is also evidence of the development of a modified version of Burke's words.

What seems likely is that the 'quotation' as it is likely to be given today is a reworking of what Burke wrote to Langrishe and the similar statement in *Reflections on the Revolution in France* (1791). The underlying thought, that a modicum at least of change is essential, is there, but the emphasis is different. The reworked version is arguably more pithy and more quotable, and is certainly more immediate ('our preservation' as against 'its conservation'). The words attributed to Burke are quoted with evidently deliberate invocation of the supposed author. What is being demonstrated is the perceived potency of Burke as an authority for a particular strand of political thought.

There are times when we can see this process applied to less literary and more recent utterances (although it may be too early to say whether a lasting formulation has really been achieved). One such instance presented itself in 2016, in relation to Tony Blair. Arriving for the Northern Irish peace talks in 1998, the then prime minister had declared: 'This is not a time for soundbites. We've left them at home. I feel the hand of history upon our shoulders.'[15] In July 2016, the House of Commons debated the Chilcot Report into the Iraq War. The Member for Foyle, Mark Durkan, asked Tony Blair's successor but one, David Cameron: 'This is not a day for soundbites, but does the Prime Minister not agree that the hand of history should be feeling someone's collar?'[16] (While neatly delivered, this was not an original coinage; in 2003, the *Mail on Sunday* reported on an anonymous woman queuing to attend the session of the Hutton Inquiry at which Tony Blair (then prime minister) was to appear: 'I want to see the hand of history on his collar.'[17]) Mark Durkan did not make overt reference to Tony Blair; presumably he felt he had no need to do so. The reference to the 'hand of history' was a rhetorical device that would have the desired effect. His confidence that the reference would be understood indicates a belief that the original words would be remembered and the allusion to their author understood. A few months later, another allusion to the same quotation appeared, but this time with a varied element in the formula. In December 2016, the *Sun* newspaper's political editor reported that a request from the ex-prime minister for further funding for Middle East travels had been turned down by the Foreign Office. The decision had been conveyed in a formal letter from the Foreign Secretary, Boris Johnson, which the *Sun* saw as 'teasing' the former prime minister by 'paraphrasing one of his famous quotes'. The quoted sentence read: 'Sadly I feel the hand of prudence on my shoulder.'[18] At this stage, the quotation is clearly 'famous' enough to be recognizable, at least within the political world, even when wordplay introduces a variable.

Phrases and Sayings

Quotations may generate an amended version that flourishes alongside the original. When looking at evidence for quotations 'on the move' I noticed an example from my childhood home—Petersfield, in Hampshire. In December 2015, the local paper reported that the Education Officer at the Petersfield Museum was moving on to a new role at the Novium museum in Chichester. Specifically, to quote the article, she was 'leaving for fresh fields and pastures new'.

Today 'fresh fields and pastures new' is little more than a cliché (it is, for instance, included in Penguin's 2007 dictionary of clichés, and correctly identified there as originating in a misquotation of a line from John Milton's *Lycidas* (1678): 'Tomorrow to fresh Woods and Pastures new.'[19] However, investigation of its history throws a light on how a quotation can generate a fixed expression that I suggest makes it of more interest than a mere mistake.

The cliché, as it is now seen, for a move to a new area of activity, has a long history. Online research quickly takes it back to well into the nineteenth century—as, for example, in Mary Russell Mitford's *Belford Regis* (1835). In the first volume, we read of Stephen Lane, the butcher and radical, who devotes his energies to political reform. He is successful, but this brings its own challenges, since his opponents give in all too readily. As a result, 'scandalised at the pacific disposition of his adversaries', he leaves the reformed borough, and turns his steps 'towards "fresh fields and pastures new"'. In the second volume, at the conclusion of 'Belles of the Ball-Room: Match-Making', a double wedding has been celebrated. We are told that 'Miss Caroline, as bridesmaid, accompanied the fair bride to "canny Northumberland", to take her chance for a husband amongst "fresh fields and pastures new"'. In both cases, the phrase is set in quotation marks, and we could be tempted to assume that it is simply a direct, if erroneous, quotation. However, against this there is no explicit reference to Milton, and the expression was not coined by Mary Russell Mitford. It appeared, for instance, in 1820, in a review of a recent French novel, *Mademoiselle de Tournon*. The article opened with a survey of the present state of France (where the reviewer purportedly saw more promise in the country's commercial and political advancement than in 'the immediate interests of her literature'). It then moved to the particular, having 'dwelt so much longer than was necessary, upon books that every one has read, that we may now turn our readers into "fresh fields and pastures new"'.[20] The phrase also appears in the 1839 preface to the first book edition of Charles Dickens's *Nicholas Nickleby*, in the 1838 'Proclamation' by 'Boz' of the forthcoming book, which announced to the public that it would be their aim to amuse by producing 'a rapid succession of characters and incidents' cheerfully and pleasantly described. To achieve this, 'we have wandered into fresh fields and pastures new, to seek materials for the purpose'.[21]

Like Mary Russell Mitford, the writer of the review of *Mademoiselle de Tournon* delineated the key phrase with quotation marks, but without any reference to a source. We therefore have no way of knowing, in either case, whether Milton was being quoted incorrectly, or whether the quotation marks are scare quotes, intended to indicate the conscious use of a non-standard expression. Dickens, however, employs the phrase as an idiom, without any typographical distinction, and there is increasing evidence for this kind of use. (One of the later and more notable ones is by James Joyce in *Ulysses*: 'Wrapped in the arms of Murphy, as the adage has it, dreaming of fresh fields and pastures new.'[22])

There is evidence of the incorrect version being used as an attributed quotation in the mid-nineteenth century. In 1841, the *Monthly Chronicle* published an article on emigration to Australia under the title 'Australind', name of the Western Australia Company's proposed settlement. Beneath the title heading appeared the words '"Tomorrow to fresh fields and pastures new."—Milton.' The misquotation appeared again towards the end of the first paragraph. 'With the vigorous in mind and body, the reasonably dissatisfied and enterprising spirits, the predominant feeling is, no doubt, "Tomorrow to fresh fields and pastures new".'[23] A similar misuse appears in *Household Words*, 1851, in an article regarding the proposed enclosure of Epping Forest. The writer concluded

ironically, and as regards his reference inaccurately, that the officials responsible for the plan might think that they were 'acting
quite poetically in saying with Milton, in "Comus", —Tomorrow
to fresh fields and pastures new"'.[24]

It is possible to say, from other (later) nineteenth-century evidence, that there was awareness of 'fresh fields and pastures new'
as a misquotation. Leigh Hunt's correspondence, edited by his
son, gives us an instance, in an account of an exchange between
Hunt and an American visitor, the Boston publisher James T.
Fields (1817–81). Fields had invited him to breakfast, but the elderly
Hunt did not feel well enough. He explained that he still hoped to
be set up 'properly again on my locomotive legs', after which he
hoped to be able to 'see everything again, and everybody'. He
added, emphasizing his regret at refusing the invitation:

> Heartily glad should I have been to say to-day, with the line in
> 'Lycidas'—
> 'Tomorrow to fresh *Fields* and pastures new.'[25]

Fields apparently picked up the misquotation, prompting a response
from Hunt two days later. In his reply, he reflected on possible
reasons for this particular misquotation, in a passage that could
suggest that the incorrect version was one that was familiar to
him, rather than something that he felt he himself had coined.
(Perhaps surprisingly, he does not seem to consider the possibility
that the coincidence of his guest's being called 'Fields' might have
occasioned the substitution of 'fields' for 'woods'.)

> Your true reading of the text in 'Lycidas' surprised me extremely,
> making me think that some account of quotations right and wrong,
> apposite and inapposite, &c., might form a curious article. Milton,

it must be owned, might have accused his misquoters of attributing tautology to him in adding fields to 'pastures', though the one word does not of necessity imply the other. I suppose the mistake originated in a certain vague feeling of the general greater applicability of the word *freshness* to fields than to woods, on account of the greater openness of the air in fields: though Milton by 'fresh' evidently meant what he did by the word 'new'.[26]

Towards the end of the nineteenth century, the altered version is commented on as something which, as well as regrettable, is also frequently encountered. In 1888, the Boston-based *Andover Review* published an article entitled 'Current Misquotations', which pointed out that Milton's line was 'almost invariably quoted,— "To-morrow to fresh fields and pastures new"'.[27] The author went on to cite a particular instance of the line being 'misquoted in the first edition of Forster's "Life of Dickens" but corrected in the second'.[28] In 1893, an otherwise favourable review in the *Academy* of biography of the seventeenth-century religious writer Nicholas Ferrar thought that on the whole the volume's 'blemishes' such as printing 'Valdis' for 'Valdes' were 'insignificant and few'.[29] However, 'more serious, almost unpardonable, is the vulgar misquotation "Fresh fields and pastures new": an error that not only spoils the harmony of Milton's lines, but makes him tautological'.

An Ngram Viewer comparison of 'fresh woods and pastures new' and 'fresh fields and pastures new' indicates that by the late nineteenth century the second version was much the most common. By the end of the twentieth century, however, there was little to choose between the two—the popularity of both having dwindled significantly, either as a consciously literary quotation or as a cliché. Perhaps interestingly, the *OED* entry for 'pasture', revised in 2005, covers it at a subsense denoting 'a field or area of thought or activity. Esp. in *pastures new* (in allusion to quot. 1638)'. This trimming-back to one key phrase suggests a further embedding into the language, as well as the loss of any dispute between the longer versions. The whole story provides an effective illustration of how a single quotation can develop its own route, and different versions, in the language.

Milton's line had decades in which to generate the twin phrase, so I find it interesting to examine another linked pair of sayings, one genuine and one altered, which have found what looks like a lasting place in a much shorter timeframe. They were both in the news in January 2017, in coverage of the 'Women's Marches' that took place around the world the day after the inauguration of Donald Trump as forty-fifth president of the United States. The *Saskatoon Star Phoenix*, for example, reported that local marchers carried 'signs with messages like "we celebrate diversity" and "well behaved women rarely make history"'.[30] The *Greenville Daily News*, on the other hand, wrote of one of the marchers from Belding, Michigan, that 'she also made signs to take on the march, emblazoned with sayings like "Well-behaved women seldom make history"'.[31] *Folio Weekly* helpfully gave a source for the saying, noting of the signs carried by a contingent from Florida in the Women's March on Washington that 'some bore famous quotes—Laurel Thatcher Ulrich's "Well-behaved women seldom make history"'.[32]

As with 'fresh woods' versus 'fresh fields', we can establish the original form and source. We also have the author's comment on the development of what has effectively become a slogan. In her 2007 book *Well-Behaved Women Seldom Make History*, Laurel Thatcher Ulrich recounts how she was emailed from California by one of her former students, telling her that 'you'll be delighted to know that you are quoted frequently on bumpers in Berkeley'.[33] As Ulrich commented, she became used 'to seeing my name on bumpers. And on T-shirts, tote bags, coffee mugs, magnets, buttons, greeting cards, and websites.'

This widespread popular fame, perhaps surprisingly, derived from a 1976 scholarly article on women whose behaviour was held up to admiration in Puritan funeral sermons.[34] The opening paragraph contained the sentence: 'Well-behaved women seldom make history.' As Ulrich explained, the line in altered form 'escaped into popular culture' when it was used as an epigraph to an informal history of American women, *From Pocahontas to Power Suits*.[35] It was included, with the 'rarely' form, in *The New Beacon Book of Quotations by Women*.[36] This led in turn to Ulrich's being asked for permission for the words to be printed on a T-shirt. Permission was given, and from that became widely disseminated (though comparatively few of those subsequently making use of the slogan asked for permission to do so). As Ulrich noted, in a passage that gives an excellent idea of the potential range of a slogan that catches the attention:

> My runaway sentence now keeps company with anarchists, hedonists, would-be witches, political activists of many descriptions, and quite a few well-behaved women. It has been featured in *CosmoGirl*, the *Christian Science Monitor*, and *Creative Keepsaking Scrapbooking Magazine*.[37]

Today, as accounts of the 2017 Women's March demonstrate, the words can be found in both forms (and may or may not be attributed to Ulrich). Both versions have substantial usage evidence behind them, exemplifying the capacity of an individual quotation to take on a life of its own within the language.

There is no question, in respect of either 'fresh woods and pastures new', or 'well-behaved women seldom make history', of what the original wording was, or where it is to be found. In another case, however, we have not only variation in working, but what appears to be an attempt by the originator to attribute coinage to another source. The London *Times* of 11 September 2015 carried an account of the discovery of early human ancestor remains in a cave in South Africa. Those excavating thought that the site was likely to be a ritualized burial site, the preparation of which might well have required the use of fire to light the way. This was surprising, since it suggested a level of complex behaviour not expected in such a 'tiny-brained hominid'. The lead scientist, Professor Lee Berger, was quoted on the hypothesis: 'There is a saying that when you eliminate the impossible whatever remains, however improbable, must be the truth.'

This 'saying' is frequently cited as a coinage by Conan Doyle for his detective Sherlock Holmes, and it is not difficult to find instances of Holmes using it (usually to Dr Watson). In *The Sign of the Four* (1890), he is already rebuking Watson for not remembering it: 'How often have I said to you that when you have eliminated the impossible, whatever remains, *however improbable*, must be the truth?'[38] In later stories he represents it as a saying rather than his own coinage, calling it variously an 'old maxim of mine' (in 'The Beryl Coronet', 1892) and 'the old axiom' ('The Adventure of the Bruce-Partington Plans', 1917).[39] There is, however, an earler usage in which Doyle (without basis in fact) attributes the formulation to another famous fictional detective, Edgar Allan Poe's Auguste Dupin. In the short story 'The Fate of the Evangeline' (published in 1885), an ingenious explanation for the disappearance of a yacht off the Hebrides was supposedly criticized in the press as 'manifestly absurd':

It would be well, the 'Scotsman' concluded, if those who express opinions upon such subjects would bear in mind those simple rules as to the analysis of evidence laid down by Auguste Dupin. 'Exclude the impossible', he remarks in one of Poe's immortal stories, 'and what is left, however improbable, must be the truth.'[40]

Conan Doyle's affection for 'eliminate the impossible', and the ways in which he represents it, create a situation in which the expression may be understood and used as either a quotation or a saying, and when used as a quotation might be attributed either to himself or to Holmes, or (incorrectly) to Poe or Dupin. This is an item that has been 'on the move' since its inception.

Out of Context

Variation in wording is an obvious way for a quotation to change, but it is also possible for the wording to be constant, and the sense to vary. A quotation is frequently excerpted from a longer passage, and as such may well be used in a different context from its original one—something that is part of a quotation establishing its own existence. On occasion, however, when the excerpted material is presented as what its original author intended to say, there may be objections. An inscription on the Martin Luther King memorial in Washington DC provides a striking (although now excised) example.

In September 2016, *Forbes* magazine published a survey of a number of monumental restorations in Washington DC.[41] The Martin Luther King Memorial had in fact been completed only in 2011, but restoration was necessary to remove one of the original features. The monument included a granite statue of King 'flanked by cherry blossoms and a wall of his famous quotes' by the Chinese sculptor Lei Yixin. However, objections to the context of one of the quotations inscribed there had led to its elimination by the Department of the Interior (at a cost, according to this piece, of between $700,000 and $900,000).

Five years before, in September 2011, the *Washington Post* published an op-ed piece by Rachel Manteuffel under the heading 'A Monumental Misquote on the Martin Luther King Jr Memorial'.[42] The editorial noted a fortunate aspect of the postponement in August, due to Hurricane Irene, of the official dedication of the Martin Luther King Jr National Memorial. It would allow those in charge to use the extra time 'to do some erasure and re-inscription of the quotation on the side of the main sculpture—and this time get it right' (see Figure 17).

At issue were the words 'I was a drum major for justice, peace and righteousness'. The source was Martin Luther King's last sermon, 'The Drum Major Instinct', given on 4 February 1968. As the editorial pointed out, the thrust of the sermon was to warn his congregation against the dangers of self-promotion and the desire to outdo others—a drive summed up in the phrase 'the drum major instinct'.[43] What mattered was to put your energy into serving others, not in trying to seem better than them, and not in seeking accolades for good works. As the editorial put it:

> Notably, he sought no such accolade for himself. 'If you want to say I was a drum major,' he said, 'say that I was a drum major for justice'. Remove that 'if'—as the architects of the monument did—and you are perversely left with the sort of bragging that Dr King decried.[44]

In January 2012 the same columnist contributed an update to the story, centring on the news that it had just been announced officially

Figure 17. Martin Luther King memorial showing the words 'I was a drum major', which were later excised.

that the quotation would be corrected.[45] (In the interim, following the original piece, there had been considerable public criticism of the excerpting, although the need to make the change was not initially accepted.) An interesting detail in the second column was the information that the original plans did include 'the full, in-context quote', but that it had later been edited on design grounds. Certainly, when the correction was made, the words were simply removed rather than any attempt being made to restore the original and longer version. This particular instance of a quotation apparently on the move may be significant in that it could be less likely in future that the truncated version will turn up as an unquestioned Martin Luther King attribution, taken out of context to give the wrong reading.

Misquotations in a public and official context are those that are most likely to be challenged. (In 2015, the issue of a commemorative stamp in honour of Maya Angelou brought to light a misattribution that had clearly gained considerable currency.[46]) Nevertheless, however conscientiously editors and readers point out that this was not what was 'really' written or said, the errant form frequently has the capacity to survive and be passed on. Thanks to modern technology and especially social media, an 'incorrect' (or completely apocryphal) quotation can gain wide recognition in a very short period. Even when a correction has been recognized and accepted, it is still probable that the form objected to will be found quoted in other circumstances.) It is, in fact, often more likely to do so, as it is also likely to be couched in pithier and more quotable terms. It is perhaps an instance of something foreseen by the Baptist preacher and religious writer C. H. Spurgeon when he wrote:

If you want truth to go round the world you must hire an express train to pull it, but if you want a lie to go round the world, it will fly; it is as light as a feather, and a breath will carry it. It is well said in the old proverb, 'a lie will go round the world while truth is pulling its boots on'.[47]

For anyone interested in quotations, misquotations are a perennial source of interest, not least because of their enduring quality. In the following chapters I shall look at further examples, moving over into the areas of direct misattribution and apocryphal quotation.

CHAPTER 7

WELL-KNOWN WORDS OF …?

O ne particular type of misquotation has produced some striking examples. In this category come instances in which a well-known person quotes from a named source, slightly altering the original. The modified version, permanently linked with the name of whoever has quoted it, then becomes a well-known quotation in its own right. Its wording may in the public mind replace the original, or coexist with it, but the dual link with two significant names has been established. In other instances, the quotation may come from a fictionalized presentation of a real person, and the quotation is then taken as genuine. To take one example, in January 2014 the author and screenwriter William Nicholson gave an interview to the *Guardian*. In his concluding remarks he said: 'As I had C. S. Lewis say in *Shadowlands*, "We read to know we're not alone." I still believe that is true.' In the film *Shadowlands* (1993) C. S. Lewis, played by Anthony Hopkins, recalls the words as said to him by a student's father; later in the film he says them again. They were created by Nicholson for the film, and do not appear in any of Lewis's writings, but it is not difficult to find them online among collections of quotations about reading, attributed without question to Lewis. Fiction in this case has overtaken fact.

Famous Saying of …?

Sometimes quotations from significant writers take on a new identity through being reworked by a famous person. The novelist Graham Greene was fond of citing an 'apothegm' he attributed to the radical Thomas Paine (1737–1809): 'We must guard even our enemies against injustice.' The words in this form are not found in Paine's writings, but they are clearly linked closely with a passage in his *A Dissertation on the First Principles of Government* (1795), in which he said: 'He that would make his own liberty secure, must guard even his enemy from oppression; for if he violates this duty, he establishes a precedent that will reach to himself.'[1] 'Guard even his enemy from oppression' is fairly clearly the origin of the later version, although the fuller passage carries an implication of enlightened self-interest that the pithier version does not express. If we compare usage evidence for the two versions, it is swiftly apparent that the 'genuine' version is better known today. In summer 2015, the adjuration to 'guard even enemies against injustice' garners under 500 Google hits; 'guard even his enemy from oppression', on the other hand, returns over 24,000 hits.[2] However, the altered version does have some usage evidence. What is the background of the lesser-known variant, and why is it more than a straightforward mistake?

The first question to ask, of course, is where the modification comes from. The alteration of 'oppression' to 'injustice' is one that might occur quite naturally. Looking for early examples, I found one of each in publications of 1918. The first appears in an article entitled 'Liberty and Freedom' by Thomas O'Shaughnessy, published in the *Overland Monthly and Out West Magazine*, September 1918. While it is not voiced as an explicit quotation, it clearly

derives from Paine. The key sentence runs: 'To make our own liberty secure, we must guard even our enemies from oppression.' The
second example appeared a few months earlier, in the *Brooklyn
Daily Eagle* of 28 July 1918, in a column about I.W.W. (Industrial
Workers of the World) members who were awaiting trial. Criticism
had been levelled at those who had contributed to a fund for their
defence, and one of the contributors was quoted in reply:

> The defense is a group of poor men who have been lying in prison
> for more than a year awaiting trial. Should not the fair-minded citi-
> zen who loves justice approve of the statement of the author of the
> Declaration of Independence that 'He who would make his own
> liberties secure must guard even his enemy from injustice'?

In this instance, we have an incorrect word ('injustice' instead of
'oppression') but a strong reference to its originator that implicitly
expects that he will be identified through a description (though
giving Tom Paine sole credit for the Declaration of Independence
may have been something of an overstatement). However, it
does mean that both versions were current in the early twentieth century.

What then happened, somewhat surprisingly, is that the version
with 'injustice' became so strongly associated with a later writer as
to appear almost as a coinage. In 1948, the British writer and critic
V. S. Pritchett published *Why Do I Write?*, a compilation of an
exchange of views on the writer's role in society between himself and
the novelists Elizabeth Bowen and Graham Greene. The words are
found in a letter from Greene to Pritchett in which he wrote:

> You remember Thomas Paine's great apothegm, 'We must take care
> to guard even our enemies against injustice,' and it is there—in the
> establishment of justice—that the writer has greater opportunities

and therefore greater obligations than, say, the chemist or the estate agent.[3]

In this letter, Greene has both altered the original passage and trimmed it—there is no expressed element of self-interest.

Why Do I Write? is an interesting book but not necessarily one with a wide circulation. Had this been the only occasion on which Greene used the 'apothegm', it might have remained within a limited circle. In the 1950s, however, he employed it again, and on a much more high-profile occasion.

In 1952, Greene travelled to New York to receive a literary award for his novel, *The End of the Affair*. On arrival, he was interviewed by a number of newspapers, including the *New York Herald Tribune*. In his biography of Greene, Norman Sherry quotes from this interview, which appeared under the headline 'Graham Greene Says US Lives in Red-Obsessed "State of Fear"'.[4] As the opening paragraph put it:

> Mr Greene arrived in New York about 2 p.m. yesterday and a few hours later when he granted an interview in his room at the Hotel Algonquin, immediately expressed concern over what he said is happening to American freedom because of the country's growing fear of Communism.

Saying that he was speaking like this because he liked America and Americans and 'this land of freedom', he went on to discuss what he saw as the growing danger of McCarthyism. He underlined what he was saying by two quotations, 'The only thing to fear is fear itself,' from Franklin Roosevelt's first inaugural address, and then 'We should guard even our enemies against injustice', which, of course, he attributed to Tom Paine. If the interview had taken place today, it would have gone out on the wire, and Greene's version of Paine's words would have been disseminated around the globe. But, even in 1952, this was probably enough to ensure that his paraphrase of Paine was widely read and duly repeated. It was certainly repeated by Greene—he used it again in 1981 when accepting the biennial Jerusalem Prize. The *Spectator* of 18 April 1981 carried an extract from his speech. In it he looked back to the 1930s, when he saw the struggle between the rights of the individual and the rights of the state as having been oversimplified to a commitment to Communism against Nazism and Fascism. In the 1980s, it was no longer a question of a simple alternative.

> There are degrees of socialism and degrees of capitalism and I hope and believe there are degrees of Communism. It is now more than ever necessary for the writer (of course I am thinking mainly of the novelist) to be uncommitted to all except the one principle of the socialist Thomas Paine—'We must guard even our enemies against injustice.'

In fact, most of the uses of the 'injustice' version of the quotation from the later twentieth century have some link with Greene: they are likely to appear either in interviews with him or in writing about him. The association has carried over into the twenty-first century, most notably in an article about the remake of the film *The Quiet American*, starring Michael Caine. Originally made in 2001, it had previewed on 10 September that year. In the aftermath of 9/11, the distributors shelved it, opening it only in the following autumn. An article by Jon Wiener, 'Quiet in Hollywood', published in the *Nation* on 16 December 2002, described the difficulties, including the reluctance to show a film that might be seen as unpatriotic. Looking at what he called 'Hollywood's self-censorship', Wiener reflected on what Greene himself would have made of it.

In so doing, he recalled Greene's visit to New York in 1952 and the interview in the *New York Herald Tribune* in which he 'quoted Thomas Paine, "We should guard even our enemies against injustice"'. To sum up, the altered version has also established a place for itself, especially in association with Graham Greene, and his demonstrable affection for the saying over several decades.

Significant Moments

Greene employed his reworking of Paine on various occasions between 1948 and 1981, in a process that reinforced the attribution of the 'apothegm' to Paine over the years. By contrast, a resonant alteration of a classical passage reached public attention on a single and very famous public occasion.

In July 2016, in the wake of the killing by rifle fire of police officers in Dallas, a columnist for the *Miami Herald* contributed a blog reflecting on the levels of violence shown in this and other recent shootings. In his piece, 'America has Gone Mad and there's no Place to Hide', he looked back to 1968, a year also marked by violence.[5] Recalling the assassination of Martin Luther King, 3 April 1968, he recounted how Senator Robert Kennedy addressed an audience in Indianapolis. His prepared speech had been discarded in response to the news of King's death, and a key passage of what he now said as he pleaded for an end to violence included a quotation. Telling his hearers that his favourite poet was Aeschylus, he quoted: 'And even in our sleep pain that cannot forget falls drop by drop upon the heart, and in our own despair, against our will, comes wisdom through the awful grace of God.'[6] The quotation turned up again in November 2016, in a column reflecting on the bitter divisiveness of the presidential election campaign. Contrasting the situation with that of the 'joyous band-wagons (literally)' of earlier elections, the columnist wrote: 'This November, we are sullen … No one sings.' Reflecting that there had been 'haunted years' before, he reminded his readers that in 1968, after hearing of the death of Martin Luther King and weeks before his own assassination, Robert Kennedy 'was quoting the Greek poet Aeschylus to an inner-city Indianapolis crowd that was ready to burn anything, as did inner cities across America, upon hearing of Martin Luther King's murder'. He went on to repeat Kennedy's quotation, emphasizing the difference between 1968 and 2016 (in which he saw 'neither poetry nor grace').

The words spoken by Kennedy in April 1968 had been widely reported at the time, with passages including the Aeschylus refer-ence.[7] Unsurprisingly, they were recalled when, in June of that year, Kennedy himself was shot and killed by an assassin.[8] They were subsequently, with one modification, engraved on the Robert F. Kennedy memorial in Arlington Cemetery, installed in 1971. The words there read: 'AESCHYLUS WROTE IN OUR SLEEP PAIN THAT CANNOT FORGET FALLS DROP BY DROP UPON THE HEART AND IN OUR DESPAIR AGAINST OUR WILL COMES WISDOM THROUGH THE AWFUL GRACE OF GOD.' 'In our despair' rather than 'in our own despair' is now a form of the quotation from Kennedy's speech for which evidence can be demonstrated. However, this is only one modification to a quotation that has undergone other changes from the original Greek. It is worth unpacking these, and following the route by which they reached Kennedy.

Happily, we are in a position to know this, thanks to Arthur M. Schlesinger Jr's biography of Robert Kennedy. In this work, he cites an interview with Jacqueline Kennedy Onassis in which she told him that in the spring of 1964 she had given her brother-in-law a copy of *The Greek Way* by the classicist and educator Edith Hamilton (1867–1963).[9] It is relevant here to note a comment on Hamilton in the *American National Biography*. The article properly pays tribute to Hamilton's gifts as a scholar and popularizer of classical civilization, whose work 'revived the study of Greco-Roman antiquity' in America. However, it also notes that in her 'elegantly written' books she was capable both of mistranslating passages and of taking them out of context.

Kennedy had read *The Greek Way* assiduously, underlining key passages. The text of the passage as he quoted it in Indianapolis appears in the book. Writing on Aeschylus, whom she called 'a great and lonely thinker', Hamilton spoke of his belief in 'the justice of God', in which the purpose of pain and error is to lead to knowledge. She then gives (with one significant difference) the passage that was to be recalled by Kennedy: 'God, whose law it is that he who learns must suffer. And even in our sleep pain that cannot forget, falls drop by drop upon the heart, and in our own despite, against our will, comes wisdom to us by the awful grace of God.' As a modern classicist, Mary Beard, has pointed out, where Kennedy 'spoke poignantly of "our own despair"', Edith Hamilton had 'in our despite', a phrase that, as Beard points out, is not only 'an archaising and accurate translation of Aeschylus' original', but has a different sense.[10] However, the resonance of Kennedy's wording, and the circumstances in which his version was coined, has fixed the form as it is now likely to be quoted. Importantly, it has also become strongly associated with Kennedy himself.

We have already seen that the words were recalled and requoted in the aftermath of the assassination of Robert Kennedy—for instance, by Arthur Schlesinger Jr in a commencement speech at the City University, New York, 5 June 1968, the day after Kennedy had been shot and killed. A striking later instance is found in Henry Kissinger's account of the last days of the Nixon presidency. In his memoir (1982), Kissinger recalled how, the night before Nixon's resignation, the president asked Kissinger to pray with him. He wrote that he hardly knew what to pray for, but that a passage from Aeschylus kept running through his mind—'the verse that, as it happened, was a favorite of one of Nixon's obsessions, Robert Kennedy'.[11] He went on to quote the lines in verse format:

> Pain that cannot forget
> falls drop by drop
> upon the heart
> until in our despair
> there comes wisdom
> through the awful
> grace of God.

In the present century, continuing the association with the Kennedy family, the lines were quoted again in the United States Senate on 10 September 2009. The occasion was the Senate's tribute to Senator Edward Moore ('Ted') Kennedy, last of the three Kennedy brothers, who had died at the end of August. In his speech, Senator Menendez told the Senate: 'In this past week, I think we have all found new meaning' in what he described as 'those familiar words of Aeschylus'. Continuing by quoting the passage that Robert Kennedy had delivered in Indianapolis in 1968, he concluded: 'Today in our despair, let wisdom come. Let us honor the memory of Senator Edward Moore Kennedy by not only remembering the man but by continuing the good that he has done.' It seems apparent that Robert Kennedy's coinage of 'in our [own] despair' had by this time become an accepted form, strongly associated with the occasion on which he used it.

This was not, in fact, the only contribution made by the speech to the wider stock of quotations 'vocabulary'. There is a second item whose route to public notice is in some ways even more interesting, and which has moved through mistaken attribution into the area of apocryphal quotations.

In September 2015, a column in the Sri Lankan *Sunday Leader* began with an attributed quotation: '"Tame the savageness of man and make gentle the life of this world." Aeschylus.' The opening paragraph ran: 'Robert F. Kennedy used Aeschylus to explain the need to make life gentler at a turbulent juncture in history in the 1960s. It is appropriate to echo this statement in light of the savageness that surrounds us evident from stories one hears on a daily basis.'[12] In the penultimate paragraph of his speech, Kennedy had pleaded: 'And let's dedicate ourselves to what the Greeks wrote so many years ago: to tame the savageness of man and make gentle the life of this world.' Perhaps understandably, given the earlier quotation from Aeschylus, these words have been taken as originating from the same source. The origin, however, is more complex—and has happily been traced in a fascinating article published in the *Classical World* in 2003.[13] The writer, Joseph Casazza, explains that the phrase 'to tame the savageness of the world and make gentle the life of the world' can also be traced back to Edith Hamilton. Crediting her with the coinage of 'to tame the savageness of man and make gentle the life of the world', he traces the history of the phrase in her writings.

She had first employed it in an article on the classics in the journal *Classical World* in 1957, the publication of a paper read to the

Classical Association of the Atlantic States (CAAS) in April of that year. As she wrote: 'There was said to have been an old inscription at Delphi which stated a man's aim is to tame the savageness of the world.' A year later, she made a similar reference to an 'old Greek inscription', in 'The Lessons of the Past', an article published in the *Saturday Evening Post*, 27 September 1958, and included as a chapter in her book *The Ever-Present Past* (1964). Casazza carefully unpicks the origin of this supposed inscription, showing that Hamilton had actually conflated two separate sources, an inscription at Delphi, and a quotation from Dionysus of Halicarnassus. He demonstrates that she appears to have derived the originals from the writings of the classicist Gilbert Murray, in *The Rise of the Greek Lyric* (second edition of 1924).

Casazza's analysis is an object lesson in tracing the roots of what was to become a resonant phrase in American political discourse, permanently associated with Robert F. Kennedy. The whole story provides a striking illustration of how 'quotations' that are in fact a construct may come into being and disseminated. It exemplifies especially the way in which material that would originally have been limited to the audience for a particular subject area (in this case, classical Greek) can make its way to a wider world through the writings of someone whose work was planned for and reached a more popular readership. The next stage was for it to be used by a significant figure on a high-profile occasion— something that both ensured its permanent place in the general vocabulary, and made possible through association with other references in the speech the occasional misattribution to Aeschylus. When we look at the journey this quotation has taken, we can see how easy it is for an individual item to take on an identity of its own.

Sometimes it is possible to see attributions being blended. In August 2016, Peter Hennessy interviewed the veteran Conservative politician Kenneth Baker for his BBC Radio series *Reflections*.[14] Looking back to 1968, when he first entered parliament, Kenneth Baker recalled various parliamentarians of the day notable for their oratory, one of whom was Iain Macleod (1913–70). Saying affectionately, 'he was a great orator, he had some lovely things to say', he went on to instance some examples. The first of these related to the devaluation crisis of 1970, when the then prime minister, Harold Wilson, had apparently claimed to be 'a very honest man'. Macleod, in Kenneth Baker's recollection, had commented: 'When the Prime Minister talks of honesty, we have to count the spoons. Wonderful way of putting it.' The second, as he recalled, was one of Wilson's junior ministers: 'There was Wedgwood Benn flying a kite, and there were we watching it thud to the ground.'

The comment on Tony Wedgwood Benn, Labour left-winger and enthusiast for technology, seems likely to have been original, but the reference to 'counting our spoons' is different. It comes from a speech Macleod made in the House of Commons debate on the Budget in April 1970, and formed the climax of a passage. The impact in fact derives not from an original coinage but from an attributed quotation used as the climax of a passage:

> Anyone who has studied the Prime Minister's undertakings, from the grammar schools, which were not to be abolished except over his dead body, no extra unemployment, no extra taxation, Rhodesia, up to the final undertaking on housing, 'not a lightly given promise but a pledge', anyone who has studied the whole range of undertakings must have evolved what we might call 'Wilson's Law', which states a great truth in simple terms: the more

definite the promise, the more certain the breach. Or, as Emerson put it a century ago: 'The louder he talked of his honour, the faster we counted our spoons.'

The reference is to a line from *The Conduct of Life* (1860), by the American philosopher and poet Ralph Waldo Emerson (1803–82), but the image can be traced back further, to the dry words of Dr Samuel Johnson, as recorded by Boswell: 'But if he really does think there is no distinction between virtue and vice, why, Sir, when he leaves our houses, let us count the spoons.'[15] Lord Baker's recollection has focused on Emerson's central image, but edited and tightened Macleod's actual usage. Where Macleod cited Emerson directly, adding that the words came from 'a century ago', Kenneth Baker adapted the words so that the unidentified 'he' became 'the Prime Minister' [Harold Wilson], and 'the faster we counted our spoons' was given immediacy by a change of tense to 'we count the spoons'.

Fiction and Reality

On occasion, what appear to be quotations from an actual writer derive from a fictionalized presentation, perhaps created by someone who is a significant writer in his or her own right. In Adam Sisman's 2015 biography of John le Carré, he recounts how in 1939 the German novelist Thomas Mann, then living in exile in America, had brought out *Lotte in Weimar*, a novel about the elderly Goethe and the woman who had been his inspiration for *The Sorrows of Young Werther*. At one point in the story, the fictional Goethe reflects on the national character of the Germans, 'in particular their susceptibility to "any mad scoundrel who appeals to their lowest instincts, who confirms them in their vices and teaches them to conceive nationalism as isolation and barbarity"'. Pointing out how relevant this passage appeared in the post-war years, Sisman goes on to note that the passage had been quoted in his closing speech at the Nuremberg trial by Hartley Shawcross, Attorney-General and chief British prosecutor at Nuremberg, in the belief that they were actually the words of Goethe.

The Times of 29 July 1946 carried the text of the Attorney-General's speech, following the report of the trial by 'Our Special Correspondent'. Under the subhead 'Goethe's Words', the following passage appears:

> Years ago Goethe said of the German people that some day fate would strike them ... 'Would strike them because they betrayed themselves and did not want to be what they are. It is sad that they do not know the charm of truth, detestable that mist, smoke, and berserk immoderation are so dear to them, pathetic that they ingenuously submit to any mad scoundrel who appeals to their lowest instincts, who confirms them in their vices and teaches them to conceive nationalism as isolation and brutality.' With what a voice of prophecy he spoke—for these are the mad scoundrels who did those very things.

The letter columns of *The Times* of 5 August 1946 carried a letter from Gustav Mayer, under the heading 'Fate and the Germans', identifying (somewhat elliptically) the true source of the quotation. He wrote that he feared that it would be difficult for Sir Hartley Shawcross 'to tell us exactly where Goethe with a "voice of prophecy", predicted to the Germans that some day "Fate would strike them". For Thomas Mann, writing after the event, it was not so difficult to put such a prophecy into the mouth of Goethe.'

A further letter under this heading was published in *The Times* of 9 August 1946. Pointing out that the Mayer letter left readers in doubt as to the origin of Shawcross's quotation, Heinrich Eisemann wrote:

> The quotation is a combination of two passages from Thomas Mann's 'Lotte in Weimar', pp. 329 and following, and 337; I quote from the first German edition printed in Stockholm, 1939. 'Lotte in Weimar' does not claim to be more than a novel, so the 'quotations' are not Goethe's own words, but a prophecy Thomas Mann put into the mouth of Goethe. When I first read the book I marked these two passages as well as a similar one on page 167 as clearly aimed at Nazi Germany.

Eisemann went on to comment that he could 'well imagine many a Goethe scholar in Germany and elsewhere has searched in vain for the passages mentioned, all the more so as the novel, written after Thomas Mann went into exile, seems practically unknown in Germany'.

In his 1995 biography of Mann, Donald Prater quoted an extended passage from *Lotte in Weimar*, beginning: 'That they [the German people] don't know the attraction of truth is regrettable, that they welcome vapourings, intoxication, and every berserk excess, repulsive—that they fall willing victims to any ecstatic rogue who can arouse their lowest instincts ...'.[16]

Prater recounts that copies of the book were smuggled into Germany during the war. Anti-Nazis 'extracted the more virulent passages and circulated them under the camouflaged title of "Goethe's Conversations with Riemer"'. He added that it was 'something of a compliment' after the war to find Shawcross quoting the words as Goethe's own. Apparently even then 'the quotations continued to be reproduced and cited, however, and it was not until 1949 that the riddle was solved in Germany'. It would seem from this, therefore, that the material was better known in Germany than Eisemann had realized, although in circumstances that made confusion of attribution likely.

Mann himself wrote about what happened in *The Story of a Novel*:

> In the long monologue of the seventh chapter there occur authentic and documented sayings of Goethe side by side with apocryphal matter of my own invention, to which, of course, I gave a Goethean cast. Opponents of the regime had extracted from this monologue a number of dicta which analysed the German character in unfavourable terms and warned that it might lead to evil; these passages had been collected and distributed as a leaflet under the camouflage title of *From Goethe's Conversations with Riemer*.[17]

A 'copy or translation of the curious forgery' had reached Sir Hartley Shawcross, who had been impressed by the 'topical forcefulness of the remarks', and who had quoted from it in good faith. As Mann recounted: 'He was not to escape unscathed.' Following critical coverage (Mann instances an article in the *Times Literary Supplement*), the Foreign Office requested Lord Inverchapel, Ambassador in Washington, to write to Mann—who agreed that *The Times* had been correct, and that the whole thing was due to a well-meant mystification on the part of the pamphleteers'. However, Mann added a caveat: 'I could warrant, I declared, that if Goethe had not really said the words the prosecutor attributed to him, he might very well have said them. In a higher sense, therefore, Sir Hartley had quoted correctly.'[18]

Graham Greene, Robert Kennedy, and Thomas Mann all remain resonant names today. However, in the next case, we have something a little different. In this instance, two quotations attributed to the Roman politician and orator Marcus Tullius Cicero (106–46 BC) seem to have reached the public through the mediation of a best-selling popular writer of the mid-twentieth century. This was the British-born Taylor Caldwell (1900–85), who in 1965 had published *A Pillar of Iron*, a novel based on the life of Cicero.

The first item to be considered was quoted (at some length) in November 2016 in the aftermath of the US presidential election, by the right-wing website *NewsWithViews.com*. The columnist Kelleigh Nelson, encouraging the then President-Elect Donald Trump to 'maintain the results of victory', used it to warn him against the dangers of compromise, with the adjuration:

> Remember the words of Marcus Tullius Cicero!
> 'A nation can survive its fools, and even the ambitious. But it cannot survive treason from within. An enemy at the gates is less formidable, for he is known and carries his banner openly. But the traitor moves amongst those within the gate freely, his sly whispers rustling through all the alleys, heard in the very halls of government itself. For the traitor appears not a traitor; he speaks in accents familiar to his victims, and he wears their face and their arguments, he appeals to the baseness that lies deep in the hearts of all men. He rots the soul of a nation, he works secretly and unknown in the night to undermine the pillars of the city, he infects the body politic so that it can no longer resist. A murderer is less to fear.'[19]

(This very long passage is more commonly found in a truncated form—for instance, in James Rothrock's 2006 account of the Vietnam War, *Divided We Fall*. The epigraph to chapter one reads: '*A nation can survive its fools and even the ambitious, but it cannot survive treason from within.—Cicero.*'[20]) It is possible to point to an actual speech in which Cicero spoke about internal treachery. In one of his speeches against Catiline, having noted that there were no longer foreign rulers likely to make war on Rome, he added:

'*Domesticum bellum manet, intus insidiae sunt, intus inclusum periculum est, intus est hostis* [The sole remaining war is on our own soil, the plots, the danger, the enemy are in our midst].'[21] However, the precise words popularly quoted (as in the epigraph in Rothrock's book) come not from Cicero's own works but from Caldwell's fictionalized character. The words are actually represented as the culmination of his final speech in the Senate before his exile, rather than as a passage from one of his speeches denouncing Catiline.[22]

The second quotation from Caldwell/Cicero relates to fiscal prudence rather than homeland security, and again is likely to be quoted today. In February 2015, *Western Journalism* published an op-ed piece entitled 'Why do we Never Learn from the Past?' In a column that namechecked a variety of politicians stretching from Churchill to Lenin, particular praise was given to a figure from the classical past. As the columnist wrote:

> Perhaps the best idea for governing was uttered over 2000 years ago by Cicero. He said: 'The budget should be balanced, the Treasury should be refilled, public debt should be reduced, the arrogance of officialdom should be tempered and controlled, and the assistance to foreign lands should be curtailed lest Rome become bankrupt. People must again learn to work, instead of living on public assistance.' I wonder if Roman leaders wish they would have listened to him.[23]

This apparent advice from Cicero has been popular in recent years, especially in the USA in political contexts. When it first surfaced as a classical quotation in need of verification, it was extremely frustrating, since we were unable to run it to earth. However, thanks to the work of others made available through the Internet, its origins are now clear, as, for instance, at the University of Texas at Austin's 'The Cicero Homepage'.[24] The quotation is given there in the form:

> The budget should be balanced, the treasury should be refilled, public debt should be reduced, the arrogance of officialdom should be tempered and controlled, assistance to foreign lands should be curtailed lest Rome become bankrupt. The mobs should be forced to work and not depend on government for subsistence.

The accompanying rubric explains some of the immediate difficulties for a classicist with the words: 'Cicero might well agree with this passage, but you'd have to explain it to him first. For instance, there was no budget to balance or assistance to foreign lands.'[25] It goes on to credit Professor John H. Collins of Northern Illinois University for tracking down the original source (Caldwell's *A Pillar of Iron*). The *Quote Investigator* site, which helpfully details usage evidence for the item, gives particular credit for popularizing the passage to Otto E. Passman (1900–88), a conservative Democrat from Louisiana who, according to his obituary in the *New York Times*, 'pursued a relentless battle against spending for foreign aid'.[26] Going back to Caldwell's text, it is notable that the passage is not in fact given as direct speech. Instead, it is given in reported speech as a summary of Cicero's views as expressed to a colleague:

> Antonius heartily agreed with him that the budget should be balanced, that the Treasury should be refilled, that public debt should be reduced, that the arrogance of the generals should be tempered and controlled, that assistance to foreign lands should be curtailed lest Rome become bankrupt, that the mobs should be forced to work and not depend on government for subsistence.[27]

By 1970, with 'arrogance of the generals' replaced by 'arrogance of officialdom', these supposed words of Cicero had already amassed a degree of usage evidence. (It may also be of interest that 'arrogance of officialdom' as a quotation by itself also has some usage— for instance, in a 2016 response to the comment that what goes wrong owing to gross negligence is never intended: 'Marcus Tullius Cicero referred to this as the "arrogance of officialdom".'[28])

It looks very much as though both these Ciceronian 'quotations' achieved their popularity and usage status because they fitted very well with the concerns of a particular area of twentieth-century politics. It may be relevant here to note that, as her entry in the *American National Biography* attests, Taylor Caldwell was not only a significant bestseller. She was also 'a lifelong conservative and virulent anti-communist', and her writings were likely to appeal to a right-wing audience. However, while Caldwell's book was the immediate source for both items, there is very little evidence of recognition of her role in providing the material. Presumably, *A Pillar of Iron* was seen as the conduit for Cicero's actual words, rather than the real source for the two passages. Added to that, Caldwell was a popular bestselling author of her day, but not a writer of lasting literary merit. After her death, her name lacked continuing resonance. Cicero was the name and reputation to be invoked. Taken together, the two instances provide an illustration of how the ground between quotation, misquotation, and apocryphal saying can shift.

My final example, beginning with a twenty-first-century study of a famous murder, also involves a once-popular and now little-read author. A recent book by Diane Janes about the 'Ightham Murder', the shooting of Caroline Luard at Ightham in Kent in August 1908, considered the case in conjunction with the 'Newcastle Train Murder' of 1910. In her account, Janes reports the words used by the judge, Lord Coleridge, passing sentence of death upon John Alexander Dickman, at Newcastle assizes, July 1910: 'In your hungry lust for gold, you had no pity upon the victim whom you slew.'

The case was a *cause célèbre* of its time, and Coleridge's words over the years were reprinted several times. The court reporter, C. H. Norman, included the final stage of the trial in his essay 'The Judges and Administration of Justice' in his 1913 book *Essays and Letters on Public Affairs*. (Norman, who believed that Dickman had been wrongly convicted, was not an admirer of Coleridge.) Janes finds no merit in the view, but suggests that a side effect of his campaign was to ensure that the judge's formulation achieved longevity. That they achieved some resonance is demonstrated in *The House that Berry Built* (1945), by Dornford Yates.[29]

The story, a humorous romance with a murder story embedded, is narrated by the character Boy Pleydell, effectively an alter ego for Yates in terms of his supposed professional background. At the end of the book, Boy and his sister Daphne discuss the double murderer of the story, and Daphne expresses some pity for the dead man. Boy thinks that she has a point, but is not entirely persuaded. As he reflects to himself: 'All the same, I could not forget the words I had heard a judge use, when he was about to sentence a convict to death. "In your hungry lust for gold, you had no pity for the victim whom you slew."'[30] Before he made writing his career, Yates had been called to the Bar. He was a pupil in Treasury Chambers in 1910, the year of the Train Murder, and it is clear that his memory of a number of cases did feed into his fictionalized memoirs. He knew Lord Coleridge. As a member of the South-Eastern Circuit, he was unlikely actually to have been present in Newcastle to hear Coleridge's words, but they could have been repeated to him. In any case, he remembered and reused them, decades after they had first been said, putting them into the mouth of Boy Pleydell in effective condemnation of the man who had selected and killed an unlucky victim. The popularity of Yates's writing at the time makes it probable that Coleridge's condemnatory words reached a wider audience—albeit one that would not have recognized the genuine base of the words.

CHAPTER 8

THEY NEVER SAID IT

Apocryphal quotations are often creations attached to a real or fictional person, which are thought to reflect the public character of that person. One well-known instance was evoked in a television review of January 2017, when a critic wrote: 'Sherlock is now Britain's biggest drama. Elementary, my dear viewers.'[1] He was, of course, referring to Sherlock Holmes's supposed dampening riposte to Dr Watson, 'Elementary, my dear Watson', which was not in fact said by Holmes in any of Conan Doyle's stories. The nearest he came to it was an exchange in 'The Adventure of the Crooked Man' (1893 in *The Strand Magazine*), in which Watson's admiring 'Excellent!' receives the response of 'Elementary'. (Holmes then elaborates by explaining his achievement as an instance of the reasoner's producing what seems a remarkable effect because the other person 'has missed the one little point which is the basis of the deduction'.)

The *Quote Investigator* site, which shows the development in the public vocabulary of what was to become a classic apocryphal 'quotation', comments that 'the phrase was synthesized by the readers and enthusiasts of the legendary detective and assigned to him', and this seems a very fair judgement. The words enshrined what was seen as part of the essential relation between the brilliant

Holmes and the slower Watson—typical of the way in which an apocryphal quotation may evolve to reflect a particular persona.

Factitious Witticisms

The process by which apocryphal sayings are crafted and attributed was described by the playwright and composer Noël Coward in a diary entry for 1955. He asserted that the only thing that really saddened him was that he would not be there to read the 'nonsense' that would be written about him. 'There will be list of apocryphal jokes I never made and gleeful misquotations of words I never said. What a pity I shan't be here to enjoy them!'[2]

Looking at a slightly earlier period, the *Oxford English Dictionary* has entries for both 'Goldwynism' ('a witticism uttered by or typical of' the American film producer Samuel Goldwyn, 1882–1974), and 'Spoonerism' ('an accidental transposition of the initial sounds, or other parts, or two or more words', deriving etymologically from the name of the college head William Archibald Spooner (1844–1930)). The *ODNB* entry for Spooner devotes a paragraph to apocryphal Spoonerisms, with specific examples. What is described as 'the most famous example, "Kinquering Kongs their titles take"', is said to have no apparent foundation in fact. Others, such as 'you have hissed my mystery lectures' are 'evidently student inventions'. Similarly, Fred Shapiro in the *Yale Book of Quotations* demonstrates that various famous sayings attributed to the producer were either reworked originals that had been '"improved", like many other Goldwynisms' (for example, 'a verbal contract isn't worth the paper it's written on'), or completely apocryphal ('I can answer you in two words, Im possible', an anonymous joke in a humorous magazine that was 'pinned' on Goldwyn by another producer).

The world of politics inevitably offers a fruitful field for apocryphal quotations, and the usage history of one example is illuminating. In September 2015, with the election for a new leader of the Labour Party under way, the columnist Boyd Tonkin wrote a piece entitled 'Do Modern Leaders Need "Charisma"?' In it, he reflected on Clement Attlee, swept into office in the Labour landslide of 1945, 'after voters decided that Winston Churchill's weapons-grade charisma had done its job and could be safely retired'.[3] He went on to say that his readers might have heard a familiar story attributing to Churchill the jibe that 'an empty taxi drew up outside Number Ten, and Attlee got out'. They might also have heard of Churchill's specific rejection of the attribution, made to his private secretary John Colville:

> Mr Attlee is an honourable and gallant gentleman, and a faithful colleague who has served his country well at the time of her greatest need. I should be obliged if you would make it clear whenever an occasion arises that I would never make such a remark about him, and that I strongly disapprove of anybody who does.[4]

Kenneth Harris's biography, in which the story was told, was published in 1982, but the supposed quotation had been long recognized as apocryphal—something that did not necessarily affect its usage. Early instances, in fact, show how it developed a level of coded significance. In 1954, the *New Statesman* reviewed Attlee's memoir *As It Happened* (1954), and gave a vivid picture of how this kind of attribution can circulate, with the 'quotation' functioning as a kind of code.

There is the story, so perfectly placed in its setting by Angus Wilson in *The Wrong Set*, of the dreary, narrow, insecure failure from the minor public school, who entertains his cronies in the saloon bar by telling of the 'empty taxi which drew up at Number 10 and out stepped Mr Attlee'. That story, besides being ugly and malicious, is absurd; for Mr Attlee has never been a nobody. Yet it gained wide currency in the golf clubs and motor-car showrooms during the period of the Labour Government.[5]

The 'wide currency' among a particular set indicates a coded use. Someone repeating it approvingly would be signalling acceptance of a certain set of values.

Angus Wilson's *The Wrong Set* was published in 1949, and he uses the supposed quotation ('the Major's got a good one about Attlee') to characterize the right-wing Trevor, who dislikes foreigners as much as the Labour government.[6] The effect is strengthened by the depiction of Trevor as someone who employs a surface politeness ('perfect manners' thinks another character) to mask actual feelings. He is shown as being affable to Mr Pontresoli, although what he really thinks of him has been expressed earlier to his friend Vi as 'filthy wop'. Nearly twenty-five years later, Howard Brenton and David Hare used the 'empty taxi' as part of their characterization of the Conservative councillor and estate agent James Avon in their play *Brassneck* (1973): 'I hear when the Election result was declared, an empty taxi drew up outside 10 Downing Street, and Mr Attlee got out.'[7] The earliest instance of attribution of the jibe to Churchill that I have found comes in a translated source of 1968, André Fontaine's *History of the Cold War*.[8] According to this book, Attlee 'cut so unremarkable a figure that Churchill once said cuttingly of him: "One day an empty taxi stopped in Downing Street. A man got out. It was Attlee."' Much nearer our own time, Andrew Marr in his *History of Modern Britain* reflected on how the jibe was used in hostile references to the new prime minister: 'He was the butt of some often retold Churchillian insults: "An empty taxi drew up at the House of Commons and Attlee got out" (though Churchill later denied that one).' The point of this 'quotation' was to be dismissive of the incoming premier who had defeated Churchill, and it would naturally be shared among and enjoyed by those who felt themselves to have been dispossessed.[9]

It seems clear from Harris's account that the attribution to Churchill in oral tradition at least was contemporary, but where else can it be found in printed sources in English before 1982? It was in fact included uncritically in the political journalist James Margach's *The Abuse of Power* (1978), describing Fleet Street's mockery of Attlee. 'Churchill, too, joined in. "An empty taxi pulled up at No. 10 and Attlee got out," he quipped.' Four years later the authoritative disavowal of Churchill's authorship of the quip appeared in Kenneth Harris's biography.

Was it, then, simply a manufactured quotation, coined to fit an occasion and express political rancour? There is evidence to suggest something a little more interesting. An American book published in 1951, Green and Laurie's *Show Biz from Vaude to Video*, included a section on the 1920s. In this, Green and Laurie described the actors' strike of 1919, led by the Actors' Equity Association.[10] The actor-managers George Cohan and Louis Mann had founded the Actors Fidelity League, which opposed many of Equity's demands. After the strike had been settled on terms favourable to Equity, there was some resentment. Cohan was to some extent exempted, but Mann and others became the subject of 'intra-trade barbs'. One of these is particularly apposite. 'It was at this time that the wheeze was cradled, "An empty taxi drew up in front of the Friars Club and Louis Mann got out.'"

Green and Laurie were looking back to the 1920s. I have not (so far) found a contemporary use of the line, but it turns out that the formula was employed by Carl Sandburg in his long prose-poem *The People, Yes*, published in 1936.[11] In the introductory passage, Sandburg notes that he includes 'sayings and yarns'. In the main text we find the verse:

> And why shouldn't they say of one windbag in
> Washington, D.C., 'An empty taxicab drew up to
> the curb and Senator So-and-So stepped out'?

Evidence that, at least across the Atlantic, the 'empty taxi(cab)' formula for mocking the insignificance of a supposedly substantial figure had already been established before the Second World War. The process then becomes the familiar one of a saying being attached to a particular figure (or, in this case, two figures, Churchill as speaker and Attlee as the subject of mockery).[12]

Accidental Associations

Sometimes what we are dealing with is a simple mistake rather than something that has been deliberately crafted or reworked for attribution. Something with a known origin is mistakenly attributed to the wrong person, and the misattribution then establishes itself in the public mind. The words 'you cannot strengthen the weak by weakening the strong' are often wrongly attributed to Abraham Lincoln. In fact, they were written by the American Presbyterian minister William J. H. Boetcker, in a 1916 publication,

'Lincoln on Private Property'. The original leaflet had Lincoln's words on one side and Boetcker's on the other, but later reprints missed out Boetcker's name, and the words were accordingly taken to be Lincoln's own.

In some instances, tracing the path of a misattribution can suggest how it has occurred. One example of this is the injunction: 'Do not follow where the path may lead. Rather go where there is no path and leave a trail.' This is frequently attributed to Ralph Waldo Emerson, and the *Oxford Dictionary of Quotations* correspondence files at Oxford University Press, as well as the *Quote Investigator* site, record appeals for verification. The attribution can now be found very widely online, especially in post-2000 sources (it also occurs in the form 'where the path leads'). Before that, it turns up as an unattributed saying or inspirational 'quotation', as in the *Virginia Journal of Science* of 1976: 'We must do as the following anonymous poem says. Do not follow where the path may lead. Go, instead, where there is no path and leave a trail.'

In 2010, when the Oxford editors for quotations first received an enquiry about verifying the origins of this quotation, online searching did not reveal anything before 1976. The first attribution to Emerson came in 1992. However, in the ensuing six years more material has become digitally available, leading researchers to earlier uses (especially in a medical and dental context), and ultimately to a poem by Muriel Strode published in 1903. The process seems to have been as follows.

In August 1903, 'Wind-Wafted Wild Flowers', a poem by Muriel Strode, was published in the *Open Court*, an American periodical with the subtitle 'a monthly magazine devoted to the science of religion, the religion of science, and the extension of the religious parliament idea'. The first line of the poem ran: 'I will not follow where the path may lead, but I will go where there is no path, and I will leave a trail.' Two years later, Strode published *My Little Book of Prayer*, in which the words appeared on their own as one of the prayers.[13] Subsequently it was quoted (with attribution) on several occasions, but one instance is of particular interest. The dedication page to Henry Ling Taylor's 1909 *Orthopedic Surgery for Practitioners* (1909) included two quotations:

> 'I look on that man as happy, who, when there is a question of success, looks into his work for a reply.'—Emerson.
> 'I will not follow where the path may lead, but I will go where there is no path, and I will leave a trail.'—Strode.

Is this, perhaps, the origin of the misattribution to Emerson, once the text became available online? A Google Books 'snippet view' gave:

> TO CHARLES FAYETTE TAYLOR PIONEER 'I look on that man as happy, who, when there is a question of success, looks into his work for a reply.'—EMERSON. 'I will not follow where the path may lead, but I will go where there is no path …'

I suggest tentatively that this may have been misread as an attribution of the words to Emerson. It would explain why, after decades of being cited as an anonymous quotation or a saying (presumably as Strode's name was forgotten), it was suddenly attached to the much-better-known writer. In its present form, it is much more likely to be cited as a direct injunction, 'do not follow …'—arguably, Strode's long-forgotten quotation has generated a modern saying.

Too Good to Be True?

In May 2016, the journal *Computer Dealer News* carried an article on what is required when entering a new sales territory. The writer suggested that it would be of benefit to consider the experiences of the early twentieth-century Antarctic explorer Sir Ernest Shackleton. The writer went on to outline Shackleton's key actions in setting up his second expedition after his first had 'ended in abysmal failure': 'To attract the right prospects, he ran the following ad: "*Small wages, bitter cold, long months of complete darkness, constant danger, safe return doubtful. Honour and recognition in case of success.*"' He received more than 5,000 replies.[14]

This advertisement has become famous as an encapsulation of disadvantages packaged in order to attract, and a Google search suggests that 'safe return doubtful' has a degree of recognition in terms of exploration. However, it also appears to be apocryphal. In 1988, John Maxtone-Graham used it as a title of a book on 'the heroic age of polar exploration'. In the preface, he quoted the supposed advertisement in full: 'MEN WANTED FOR HAZARDOUS JOURNEY. LOW WAGES. BITTER COLD. LONG HOURS OF COMPLETE DARKNESS. SAFE RETURN DOUBTFUL. HONOUR AND RECOGNITION IN THE EVENT OF SUCCESS.'[15] Noting that it crops up repeatedly as a prize-winning entry in advertising anthologies, admired for its 'deadly frankness', he goes on to say that unfortunately 'the advertisement is as spurious as it is famous'. This is substantiated by online searching, which reveals that, despite industrious efforts, no one has ever traced this advertisement. Its earliest appearance known to date is in a 1944 book *Quit You Like Men* by the American Presbyterian minister Carl Robert Elmore. Five years later, it received the accolade of inclusion in a collection entitled *The 100 Greatest Advertisements* by Julian Lewis Watkins. Under the heading 'Wanted: Volunteers for the South Pole', the supposed Shackleton advertisement was the first example given. In his commentary, Watkins wrote: 'Of course, the lure of adventure had a great deal to do with the success of this simply written copy. So did the power of deadly frankness.'

Following its appearance in Watkins's book (first published in 1949, with a second edition ten years later), the Shackleton advertisement turned up in a number of books on advertising—and from there seems to have made its way into the world from which it was supposed to come. John Maxtone-Graham's prefatory material neatly explains the process whereby an apocryphal quotation can establish its own authenticity. Writing of the advertisement he says: 'The conditions it implies, as well as the spirit it conveys, are so hauntingly evocative that I extracted from it the title for this book.'

Mysterious Origins

'The only thing necessary for the triumph of evil is for good men to do nothing' is an assertion widely ascribed (in slightly varying forms) to the writer and politician Edmund Burke. It is not too strong a statement to say that extraordinary efforts have been made to authenticate it (they are set out in particular detail at the *Quote Investigator* site[16]). The conclusion, however, is that the nearest thing that can be found in Burke's writings is a passage from his reflective 1770 pamphlet *Thoughts on the Cause of the Present Discontents*: 'When bad men combine, the good must associate;

else they will fall, one by one, an unpitied sacrifice in a contemptible struggle.' And this is not really so close, since the focus (what will happen to the good men) is rather different from the concern about a successful outcome for bad intent. Since the sixth edition of 2004, the *Oxford Dictionary of Quotations* has entered the item in its 'Misquotations' section, with a cross reference to the passage from *Thoughts on the Cause of the Present Discontents*. Another cross reference calls attention to a similar thought in the writings of the English philosopher and economist John Stuart Mill (1806–73): 'Bad men need nothing more to compass their ends, than that good men should look on and do nothing'[17]—again, not a dissimilar thought but clearly not the same expression. What is evident today is that the reflection on the triumph of evil is exceedingly well known: a Google search in March 2015 resulted in over 420,000 hits. This popularity was affirmed when in 2004 we published the sixth edition of the *ODQ*. As part of our publicity, we produced a list of 'best-known' quotations (established by online testing) and asked readers to pick their favourite. The apocryphal Burke item was a clear winner.

When we look at the usage evidence for this item, the question of dating immediately throws up a significant difficulty. The earliest examples we have are recorded from the second decade of the twentieth century. The website *Quote Investigator* reports on a speech in favour of prohibition made in 1916 and using the formulation: 'It has been said that for evil men to accomplish their purposes it is only necessary that good men should do nothing.' There was no reference to Burke, and arguably this could have been an echo of Mill. It is not until 1920 that we get the first attribution, in a speech on temperance: 'Burke once said: "The only thing necessary for the triumph of evil is that good men should do nothing."

Leave the Drink Trade alone and it will throttle all that is good in a nation's life.' The occasion was the Fourth International Congregational Council held in Boston, Massachusetts, 29 June– 6 July 1920. The speaker, Sir Murray Hyslop, was a British businessman and Treasurer of the Congregational Union of England and Wales. I think it is worth noting that the speaker was British: despite the location, the citation should be classified as British rather than American usage.

After 1920, the 'quotation' appears to go underground—although one can never be quite certain of a negative in this regard. At present, however, there does appear to be a significant usage gap. There is one relevant instance in the London *Times* of 13 August 1936 in a column commenting on a pastoral letter issued by the Methodist conference: 'It is well for the Church to be brought up against the plain facts that "for bad men to get their own way it is simply necessary for good men to do nothing", and also that a great price has to be paid for the world's salvation.'[18] The relevant words are typographically distinguished as quoted material, but there is no mention of an author—it might be considered a saying or proverb rather than an individual utterance. The key words 'triumph' and 'evil' are missing.

The next occurrence is in the *Washington Post* of 22 January 1950. In the column 'Washington Affairs' the journalist Harry N. Stull wrote with concern about the District of Columbia's crime rate. Under the heading 'Indifference Fosters Gangsterism', he commented: 'This situation is best summed up in the words of the British statesman, Edmund Burke, who many years ago said, "All that is necessary for the triumph of evil is that good men do nothing."'

Up to this point, the context in which the words (as maxim or attributed quotation) appeared was broadly one of moral obligation and civic behaviour rather than the world of politics. This, however, was shortly to change.

In November of the following year, the Canadian scholar and diplomat Lionel Gelber wrote a letter to the *New York Times*, deploring the low turnout in the recent election.[19] Under the heading 'Lessons of the Election' he observed: 'Too many Americans refrained from exercising their most important democratic right … It has been well said that all that is necessary for the triumph of evil is for good men to do nothing.'[20] The words were unattributed but presented in a way that assured the reader that this was an utterance worthy of attention.

A year and a half later, in May 1953, the *New York Times* carried a piece on the dangers of McCarthyism under the byline of John Roy Carlson.[21] Reflecting on the situation, he wrote:

> I have just returned from one year's travel abroad. I doubt if a McCarthy could prosper anywhere in Europe or the Middle East as well as he has prospered in these United States during the year of my absence. I have asked myself why this should be so. Perhaps the explanation lies in Edmund Burke's acute observation: 'The only thing necessary for the triumph of evil is for good men to do nothing.'[22]

In this case, Burke's name is given, but the weight of the citation again lies on the words rather than on the association with the originator's name.

At this point, it looks as though the quotation was becoming an accepted part of political discourse (especially, perhaps, in the *New York Times*). John Lodge, the Republican Governor of Connecticut, used it in September 1954 in 'politics is everybody's business', a piece reflecting on civic duty. As he commented: 'I am impressed with Burke's famous observation that for evil to triumph it is only necessary for good men to do nothing.'

By 1956, McCarthyism was no longer a live issue, but the cold war was still in force.[23] In spring 1956 Admiral Arthur W. Radford,[24] Chairman of the Joint Chiefs of Staff, spoke to the biennial convention of the National Jewish Welfare Board at a lunchtime session held at the Waldorf Astoria, in a speech reported in the *New York Times* for 7 April 1956. He said:

> We are participants in a battle between good and evil—a struggle between light and darkness.
> The struggle is deadly. All that is necessary for evil to triumph is for good American citizens to sit back and do nothing.

As Irving Spiegel's column in the *New York Times* described it, the admiral was 'lashing at Communist doctrines and designs'. Once more though, it is worth noting, there is no name check for Burke—the key words are being employed much more as a recognized maxim than as a quotation from a significant figure. It has even reached the stage at which key elements can be modified, with 'good American citizens' substituting for 'good men'. And it continued to be chosen as a maxim—for example, in the form 'For Evil to Triumph, Good Men Need Only Do Nothing', taken as the theme of the seventieth National Congress of the Daughters of the American Revolution in 1959.

It was, then, in the 1950s that this apparent quotation established its popularity, especially in North American politics.[25] The first example I have found in Hansard, the official journal of the British parliament, is from a debate on Hungary and Eastern Europe in the House of Lords in 1957, in the aftermath of the failed Hungarian uprising: 'I think the spirit in which we should break off would be to remember a saying that All that is necessary for the triumph of evil is that good men do nothing. Perhaps if we can go on doing something, evil may not triumph.'[26] Burke was a noted parliamentarian, but there is no reference to him here: the key words are cited as proverbial. It is not until 1962 that we find the Conservative politician Dame Irene Ward, speaking in a Commons debate on the Incomes Policy on 4 July 1962, saying:

> I understand that Burke made a statement to the effect that all that was necessary for evil to triumph was for good men to do nothing. If he had been here today he might have been moved to add that, in the doing, action should be taken which is both fair and based on common sense.

But, again, Burke's name is not really being adduced in a way that adds weight and context to the words. At best, it is deployed to add a little gravitas. And Dame Irene, sensibly, gave herself a margin for error by saying that she 'understood' that Burke had made the statement.

In summary, there is good evidence that the words, often associated with Burke, were known and quoted in the 1950s and were becoming part of political discourse. A key question now must be: Where did they come from? Were they, for instance, in any of the standard dictionaries of quotations of the late nineteenth or twentieth centuries?

The answer to this seems to be no. They do not appear, for instance, in the 1896 revised edition of J. K. Hoyt's *Cyclopedia of Practical Quotations* (1896), nor in Anna Lydia Ward's 1906 *A Dictionary of Quotations in Prose*. And it is not that they ignored Burke: both collections quote liberally from his writings. Nor have I been able to find the item in Burton Stevenson's *The Home Book of Quotations* (1934) or H. L. Mencken's *A New Dictionary of Quotations on Historical Principles*, published in 1942. It looks very much as though at this point this was not, in any form, widely used or recognized.

As has been shown, it was in the 1950s and 1960s that the quotation, with an attribution to Burke, began to establish itself—perhaps because it suited the temper of the times. Its profile may also have been raised by another circumstance. The papers of President Kennedy in the US National Archives include a letter of August 1962 from Evelyn Lincoln, personal secretary to the president. Writing to a correspondent, she concluded:

> In response to your query, the President's favourite quotation is:
> 'The only thing necessary for the triumph of evil is for good men to do nothing.'
>
> —By Edmund Burke.[27]

It is entirely believable that a quotation widely used in the political sphere in the 1950s should have come to Kennedy's attention; I would also find nothing surprising in the fact that he accepted the attribution without questioning it. In any case, use of it by him is likely to have cemented its place in the public vocabulary. Subsequently, it began to appear in dictionaries of quotations.

'The only thing necessary for the triumph of evil is for good men to do nothing' first appeared in the entry for Burke in the fourteenth edition of *Bartlett's Familiar Quotations*, published in 1968. At that point it had what appeared to be a contemporary source in a letter of 1795, but regretfully this turned out to be an error.[28] Subsequent editions have fallen back on 'attributed' and the suggestion that it may be linked to the injunction from *Thoughts on the Present Discontent* that 'when bad men combine, the good must associate'. In 1992, the fourth edition of *The Oxford Dictionary of Quotations* gave similar treatment to the variant, 'It is necessary only for the good man to do nothing for evil to triumph.'

And this is very much the position as we have it today—a known and recognized apocryphal quotation, widely attributed to Burke but not found in his writings. It can be cross-referred to a 'real' Burke quotation and to a quotation by John Stuart Mill. All these are details that can be and are conveyed within the apparatus of a dictionary of quotations. However, there is no place for the background, which in some ways is the most interesting part of the picture. To recapitulate, Edmund Burke died in 1797. The first evidence to date of this attribution comes in 1920, and there are only intermittent instances until the 1950s. It then caught the fancy of a post-war world, culminating in selection as a president's favourite. We still do not know where it came from in the early twentieth century, or why it surfaced so strongly in the 1950s.

Misattributing with Authority

In 2015, the journalist Michael Ware's documentary on the Iraq War, *Only the Dead*, was reviewed by *Blurb Magazine*.[29] The review opened:

> The film takes its title from a quote attributed to Plato: 'Only the dead have seen the end of war.' And that is the perfect title for this harrowing, confronting and uncensored up close and personal look at the horrors of war from a veteran war correspondent who spent seven years in Iraq.

Other online references to 'only the dead have seen the end of war' can be even more circumspect. In January 2016, Michael

Thompson, Public Safety Commissioner for Oklahoma, discussing the implications of the phrase 'boots on the ground', wrote:

> The likelihood that we have seen our last war is dubious at best. In Gen. Douglas MacArthur's celebrated farewell speech at West Point, he famously quoted Plato as saying 'Only the dead have seen the end of war.' Regardless of the accuracy of the quote, the simple message conveyed remains true.[30]

The attribution of this to Plato is due to General Douglas Macarthur, who used it in two high-profile speeches. In 1935, MacArthur, as outgoing Army Chief of Staff, addressed a reunion of the 'Rainbow Division', which he had led in the First World War. He included the reflection: 'In the last 3,400 years only 268—less than 1 in 13—have been free from wars. No wonder that Plato, the wisest of all men, once exclaimed, "Only the dead have seen the end of war!"'[31] In 1962, MacArthur used the same words in a farewell address to the cadets at West Point, saying:

> This does not mean that you are warmongers. On the contrary, the soldier above all other people prays for peace, for he must suffer and bear the deepest wounds and scars of war. But always in our ears ring the ominous words of Plato, that wisest of all philosophers: 'Only the dead have seen the end of war.'[32]

Considering the second speech in *The Oxford Handbook of Warfare in the Classical World* (2013), the authors comment: 'Soldier-writers and writers about what soldiers now do are given to using certain themes, ideas, and figures in classical literature as touchstones, but they leave the impression of having no serious familiarity with the works they cite or use.' MacArthur's allusion to Plato is taken as a 'strange use of a phantom citation' that proves this point. It is also noted that Ridley Scott's 2001 film *Black Hawk Down* has it as an epigraph, following Bowden's book. Further instances of the quotation, as attributed to Plato, have been used as inscriptions on a wall of the Imperial War Museum and over the entrance to the Museum at West Point. It is similarly inscribed on the Mt Lebanon Veterans Memorial, Mt Lebanon, Pennsylvania. In fact (as the *Handbook* points out), the author of the words so beloved of MacArthur was not Plato at all, but the Spanish-born philosopher and writer George Santayana (1863–1952). In a collection of essays published in 1922, Santayana described hearing a group of wounded officers, in a coffee house in Oxford, singing 'Tipperary' after the news of the Armistice. They were, he said, singing because they had been reprieved—they would not have to go back to the front, and those of their friends who had survived would come home alive. Santayana sympathized, but thought they had exchanged the 'fog of war' for the 'fog of peace'. They thought they were safe, and that the war ('perhaps the last of all wars') was over. On the contrary, said Santayana: 'Only the dead are safe; only the dead have seen the end of war.'[33] It seems likely that MacArthur, himself a veteran of that war, had read and remembered the words, but forgotten the source. Did he, wishing to use them for maximum impact, deliberately borrow Plato's name, or did he simply assume that something that had impressed him so much must have come from a significant and admired source? (See Figure 18.)

The life of this quotation as an epigraph to *Black Hawk Down* is in itself of some interest. 'Only the dead have seen the end of war' does not in fact appear in Mark Bowden's 1999 book, the epigraph to which was a longer passage from Cormac McCarthy's 1985 novel *Blood Meridian*: 'It makes no difference what men think of war, said the judge. War endures. As well ask men what they think

Figure 18. General Douglas MacArthur addressing an audience.

of stone. War was always here. Before man was, war waited for him. The ultimate trade awaiting the ultimate practictioner.'[34] This grim (and perhaps too long) passage was rejected for the film, but the original choice was from another source again, a poem of T. S. Eliot's. In a review of its first showing in 2001, Richard Schickel wrote: '*Black Hawk Down* begins with a quotation from T. S. Eliot: "All our ignorance brings us closer to death." By the light of its flash-bang grenades, this movie seeks to banish some of that darkness.'[35] Rollins and O'Connor's *Why We Fought: America's Wars in Film and History* (2008) has a chapter on *Black Hawk Down*. The authors of this chapter describe the change that took place after 'high civilian and military officials' had seen the film on its opening night:

> The version they saw opened with a supertitle from T. S. Eliot's *Choruses from 'The Rock'*: 'All our ignorance brings us nearer to death' ... The version issued to the public replaced Eliot's truth with a bogus quote from Plato: 'Only the dead have seen the end of war.'[36]

The authors by implication thought poorly of the change, and the use of 'bogus' to identify the mistaken attribution devalues the substituted words. But in their original source there was nothing bogus about them. The careless attribution to Plato made thirteen years later by a famous soldier, and then carried forward, was not the fault of Santayana, whose words expressed an incontrovertible, if bleak, truth in the aftermath of the First World War.

AFTERWORD

The process of writing this book has reacquainted me with some familiar quotation 'stories', although some of the detail of Conan Doyle's maxim ascribed to Sherlock Holmes, about the elimination of the impossible, was new to me. Other instances, such as the history of 'Je suis Paris', and the background to the supposed statement by Goethe that 'any mad scoundrel' could sway the German people, have been pleasurable discoveries. It has been enjoyable to revisit some items previously studied, such as 'splendid misery'.

I find it continuingly intriguing to discover backstories for individual items. Kipling remembered the line about 'nine white wolves' coming 'over the wold' as magical words from a book of children's poetry. The identification of the immediate source is interesting in itself, but it is made doubly so by linking it back to a real incident of polar exploration. And the phrase 'butter in a lordly dish' from the biblical book of Judges functions both as a coded reference, and as an instance of a traditional translation, in the King James Version, which would be rendered very differently today. How recognizable, therefore, will it be in the future?

Any general collection of quotations (such as the *ODQ*) will include both the most established and respected sources, and more ephemeral material. In some cases, such as Mandy Rice-Davies's 'He would, wouldn't he?', what might have seemed a passing phrase has embedded itself in the public vocabulary. On the other hand, 'enough of this foolery', once a political catchphrase, has died from sight. It can only be a matter of speculation as to which twenty-first-century equivalents will stand the test of time.

'Misquotations' in their varied form will always have a particular interest for me, not least because they can demonstrate the degree to which an item assumes its own identity once it has lodged itself securely in the public consciousness. It may be pointed out quite clearly that the assertion that 'there is no enjoyment like reading' is part of the characterization of the hypocritical Miss Bingley rather than a statement of Jane Austen's own beliefs, but it is highly likely to be encountered as an unqualified statement by her. The Internet today gives us unrivalled opportunities to track down the origin of a recognized but unknown quotation; however, it is also a great help in spreading or even generating misinformation. The mistaken attribution of the advice 'do not follow where the path may lead' to Ralph Waldo Emerson may well derive from the context in which it has been encountered online.

Sometimes misattribution is helped by the supposed authority given by a famous name. General Douglas MacArthur's reference to 'Plato, the wisest of men' as the source for his mistaken attribution of George Santayana's wry reflection that 'only the dead have seen the end of war' surely had a good deal to do with the establishment of that mistaken attribution. In other cases, the resonance of once-famous names has largely faded, while their (genuine) sayings have endured. The Cardinal de Retz's political influence in seventeenth-century France made him a significant figure to David Hume and Adam Smith, but his name is likely now to be remembered only in a historical context. However, the dictum that 'it is even more damaging for a minister to say foolish things than to do them' may in the era of social media strike a curiously contemporary ring.

Some stories, frustratingly, remain incomplete. The apocryphal statement that for 'the triumph of evil' it is only necessary 'for good men to do nothing' attributed (in varying forms) to Edmund Burke has been firmly established in the public vocabulary of quotations for over sixty years. However, there is an instance recorded from the first part of the twentieth century. When was it actually coined, and why did it surface when it did? Are there uses in the intervening decades that have not yet come to light?

In January 2018, *The Darkest Hour*, a film about the immediate aftermath of Churchill's becoming Prime Minister, was released in Britain. In the closing scenes, Gary Oldman as Winston Churchill wins over a previously sceptical House of Commons with his famous 'We shall never surrender' speech. His political rival Lord Halifax, watching from the gallery, tells a friend that he has 'mobilized the English language and sent it into battle'. Used in wry acknowledgement of what has occurred, this fits perfectly into the film. It is also genuine in that the words were spoken of Churchill's oratory in war. However, they were said not by Halifax in 1940, but by the American broadcaster and journalist Edward R. Murrow, speaking of Churchill in 1954. On one level, therefore, there is an error—but since it works so well dramatically, it is arguably much more interesting than a simple mistake. As a summary of the importance of Churchill's speeches at the time, it might be seen as a legitimate borrowing for dramatic purposes.

As I said in the Preface to this book, there is always another story to unpack.

NOTES

Introduction

1. For example, Garber (2003). See also de Brabanter (*c.*2005).
2. It was concluded, correctly, that she had spoken them at the committal proceedings against Stephen Ward at Marylebone Magistrates' Court, 29 June 1963 (as reported in the London *Times*, 1 July 1963, p. 6).
3. *Guardian* (online edition), 7 May 2016.
4. Otto von Bismarck, speech to the Reichstag, 5 December 1876, quoted in *ODQ* (2014: 115).
5. Letter to Norman Bottomley, Deputy Chief of Air Staff, 29 March 1945; Hastings (1979: 344).
6. John Biffen on the Foreign Secretary Malcolm Rifkind's statement on Srebenica: 'Does he ever reflect on the wisdom that echoes down the ages in Bismarck's comment that the Balkans were not worth the bones of a single Pomeranian grenadier?' (House of Commons, 12 July 1995).
7. Robert F. Kirchubel, 'V-E Day Celebrations Explain Past, Present Events in Ukraine', *San Francisco Chronicle* (online edition), 7 May 2015.
8. Fintan O'Toole, *Guardian* (online edition), 1 February 2016.
9. Reported in *Westmeath Independent* (online edition), 10 February 2016.
10. *Guardian* (online edition), 22 April 2016; possibly an allusion to the caption of Peter Steiner's 1993 *New Yorker* cartoon, 'On the Internet, nobody knows you're a dog'.
11. *Daily Telegraph* (online edition), 3 February 2009.
12. *Daily Express* (online edition), 25 May 2011.

Chapter 1

1. Cooper (1578), introduction.
2. Mencken (1942: p. v).
3. Bysshe (1702).

4. *ODNB*'s entry for Bysshe notes that 'the majority of the poetry and drama quoted in Richardson's novels is drawn from Bysshe'.

5. *Toronto Sun* (online edition), 21 November 2016.

6. See further Knowles (2009).

7. Hancher (2003).

8. e.g. Gent (1952).

9. Hancher (2003: 20), quoting from 'Reminiscences of John Bartlett', *Proceedings of the Cambridge Historical Society*, 1 (1906), 71.

10. Hancher (2003: 21).

11. Bohn (1881).

12. Unacknowledged quotation from Bacon, example of a 'canonical' quote that has dropped largely out of use.

13. *The Times* (Times Digital Archive), 9 July 1964.

14. Obituary of Sir Michael Fox (1921–2007), *Daily Telegraph* (online edition), 14 April 2007.

15. Rees (1997: 7), introduction. See also Rees (2006).

16. *Observer*, 18 March 1906, 'Sayings of the Week', p. 4.

17. 'Enough of this foolery, Timms, and come to the point' (Cooper 2009: 145).

18. Henry Campbell-Bannerman, speech in the House of Commons, 12 March 1906.

19. *The Times* (Times Digital Archive), 13 March 2006.

20. Andrew Bonar Law, speech in the House of Commons, 30 March 1909.

21. Lord Newton, speech in the House of Lords, 14 May 1906.

22. Lord Castlereagh, speech in the House of Commons, 25 February 1907.

23. A. J. A. Morris, 'Bannerman, Sir Henry Campbell- (1836–1908)', *ODNB*.

24. Justin Webb, 'Enough of this Foolery', in *Justin Webb's America* (blog), 18 May 2008, <www.bbc.co.uk> (accessed October 2016).

25. Squire (1921: 167).

26. *Week-End Review*, 19 March 1932, p. 364.

27. Humphrey Sumner Milford (1877–1952), publisher, manager of the London business and Publisher to Oxford University 1913–45.

28. The chosen volume was apparently the fifth edition of Hoyt and Ward's *Cyclopaedia* (1883).

29. H. S. Milford, letter, 26 January 1915; OUP Archives (OP1167/008658). It is not clear what Milford meant by this, since the keyword index is in expectable alphabetical sequence. Possibly what he wanted was an index of quotations ranked by the first significant word.

30. Robert William Chapman (1881–1960), literary scholar and publisher, Secretary to the Delegates 1920–42. Kenneth Sisam (1887–1971), Anglo-Saxon scholar and publisher, Assistant Secretary 1922–42, and Secretary 1942–8.

31. R. W. Chapman, letter, 10 November 1931; OUP Archives (OP1167/008658).

32. It identified the main competitors as *Bartlett's Familiar Quotations*, then in its tenth edition, W. Gurney Benham's *Cassell's Book of Quotations, Proverbs and Household Words* (1912), and Hoyt's *New Cyclopedia of Practical Quotations* (revised and enlarged by Kate Louise Roberts in 1922).

33. F. Page, 'Dictionaries of Quotations: A Survey', 24 November 1931; OUP Archives (OP1167/008658).

34. R. W. Chapman, letter, 30 November 1931; OUP Archives (OP1167/008658).

35. K. S. Sisam, letter, 27 November 1931; OUP Archives (OP1167/008658).

36. K. S. Sisam, letter, 27 November 1931; OUP Archives (OP1167/008658).

37. The importance of the American market was somewhat grudgingly acknowledged ('We must consider the Americans lovingly'), but in reality this was more likely to mean American authors regarded as having honorary status in English literature than something offering a true reflection of American culture.

38. This was 'the constantly recurring trouble with all our books nowadays' (H. S. Milford, letter, 3 March 1942; OUP Archives (OP1167/008658).

39. G. Cumberlege, letter, 17 January 1949; OUP Archives (OP1167/008658).

40. H. S. Milford, letter, 19 January 1949; OUP Archives (OP1167/008658).

41. Minutes of the 13th Meeting of the Oxford Dictionary of Quotations Committee, 8 September 1949; OUP Archives (OP1167/008659).

42. These were subsequently reduced to six in the fourth edition of 1992; in the eighth edition (2014), the total stands at five, with a cross reference to 'the lady's not for turning' as spoken by Margaret Thatcher.

43. Marghanita Laski, 'Notes on Revision of Dict. Quot.', 7 June 1970; OUP Archives (OP1168/008661).

44. OUP Archives (OP1168/008661).

Chapter 2

1. Bamborough (2012).
2. Wood (1971: i. 627).

3. Thomas Hearne, journal, 23 January 1733/4, in Hearne (1869: iii. 113).

4. For a consideration of this phenomenon, see Morson (2011), ch. 11, 'The Anthology as Literature', pp. 224–35.

5. Thackeray (1994: 422).

6. Bulwer-Lytton (2010: 64).

7. *Notes and Queries*, 2 February 1850, p. 222.

8. *Notes and Queries*, 9 February 1850, p. 233. James H. Friswell (1825–78), a professional writer, was to publish his own dictionary of quotations, *Familiar Words*, in 1865.

9. Lord Tennyson, 'The Princess' (1847): 'jewels five-words-long | That on the stretch'd forefinger of all Time | Sparkle for ever' (Tennyson 2000: 139).

10. Guy de la Bédoyère, quoted in Higgins (2013: 196). As has already been suggested, owners of the *Oxford Dictionary of Quotations* are more likely to stick with 'their' edition of the *Dictionary* than to replace it with a later version.

11. Bülow (1931: 126).

12. Edmund Ruffin, journal, 30 January 1857, in Ruffin (1857: 249).

13. *Washington Post*, 12 February 1911.

14. Moon (1989: 63).

15. Bennett (2007: 24).

16. Robert Frost, 'The Road Not Taken' (1916), quoted from *ODQ* (2014: 331).

17. Mortimer (1987: 527). I am grateful to Joseph Kennedy of Oxford University Press for bringing this story to my attention.

18. See n. 10.

19. *The Times*, 28 February 1974.

20. *The Times*, 8 March 1974.

21. Garber (2003: 121).

22. *Chicago Sun-Times* (online edition), 20 January 1999.

23. For a further discussion of the usage history of these lines, see Chapter 4.

24. *The Times*, 3 October 1961.

25. *Washington Post* (online edition), 6 April 2015.

26. Anglund (1968: 15).

27. Remarks made at the presentation of the National Medal of Arts and National Humanities, 28 July 2014.

28. *New York Times* (online edition), 8 April 2015.

29. Paul Laurence Dunbar, 'Sympathy', in Dunbar (1997: 28).
30. John Webster, *The White Devil* (1612), quoted in ODQ (2014: 815).

Chapter 3

1. Jay (1996: p. iv).
2. Dorothy Parker, 'A Pig's-Eye View of Literature' (1937), quoted in ODQ (2014: 584).
3. See entry for Mahatma Gandhi in ODQ (2014: 335).
4. Peter Lewis, *Mail Online*, 2 August 2012.
5. Interview with Gore Vidal in Plimpton (1998: 430).
6. *Washington Post* (online edition), 21 November 1982.
7. *Quote Investigator* <www.quoteinvestigator.com> (accessed 13 February 2016).
8. Abraham Lincoln, first Inaugural Address, 4 March 1861, quoted in ODQ (2014: 481).
9. Aaron Sorkin, 'These Crackpots and their Women', *The West Wing*, series 1, first shown 20 October 1999.
10. Austermühl (2014: 5).
11. Rex Tillerson, opening statement to Senate Secretary of State Hearing, 11 January 2017.
12. *Spiked* (online edition), 1 October 2015.
13. Michael White, Labour conference diary, *Guardian* (online edition), 30 September 2015.
14. *Guardian* (online edition), 29 September 2015.
15. Reported in <www.bbc.co.uk> (accessed 17 December 2017).
16. Peter Popham, *Independent* (online edition), 3 May 1997.
17. Bell (2009: 233).
18. Billy Bragg, quoted in *Financial Times* (online edition), 30 September 2000.
19. Patrick Wright, *Guardian Review* (online edition), 9 April 2005.
20. *Guardian* (online edition), 15 April 2016.
21. Andrew Marr, *New Statesman*, 1 July 2016.
22. *Time* (online edition), 8 February 2013.
23. *Time* (online edition), 18 February 2014.
24. *Sun* (online edition), 14 November 2015.
25. *Daily Mirror* (online edition), 7 December 2015.
26. *Le Figaro*, 27 November 1870, <http://gallica.bnf.fr> (accessed 17 February 2016).

27. Maud (1918: 923).
28. *Voice of America* (online edition), 30 November 2015.
29. Quoted in Petrey (1980: 110).
30. *Docklands and East London Advertiser* (online edition), 14 October 2016.
31. Piper (1964: 265). He is less than complimentary about the monument itself, reporting that it 'has been claimed as the ugliest in the city'.
32. Woolf (1992: 319).
33. *The Times* (Times Digital Archive), 17 March 1920.
34. For an account of the memorial, and its unveiling, see *The Times*, 13 October 1916.
35. See Malvern (2004: 227). The words were adduced early on to the pacifist cause. In December 1915, 'patriotism is not enough' was used by Herbert Cole in a cartoon depicting a crucifixion and the world ruined by capitalist greed in the form of Mammon, published in Sylvia Pankhurst, *Woman's Dreadnought*, 18 December 1915.
36. *New Statesman*, 10 April 1920, p. 15.
37. John Middleton Murry, 'Memorial or Incubus?', *Nation*, 27 March 1920, p. 890.
38. Shaw (1995: 523).
39. John McCain, *Politico*, 21 April 2016.
40. *The Times* (Times Digital Archive), 27 July 1864.
41. Viscount Cecil of Chelwood (1864–1958), formerly Lord Robert Cecil, politician and peace campaigner, was awarded the Nobel Peace Prize in 1937.
42. Kurt Georg Kiesinger (1904–88), lawyer and politician, Chancellor of the Federal Republic of Germany 1966–9.
43. Lyndon Baines Johnson, speech, 15 August 1967, in Public Papers of the Presidents of the United States, Lyndon B. Johnson, 'Toasts of the President and Chancellor Kiesinger of Germany', p. 349.
44. *Washington Post* (online edition), 28 January 2016.
45. Ronald Reagan, broadcast from the Oval Office after the loss of the space shuttle *Challenger* with all its crew, 28 January 1986.
46. Noonan (1990: 257). A less moving, but also interesting, account of the speech-writer's engagement with quotations is given in the story in Chapter 4 of how the biblical 'faint in the day of adversity' was found for and used by Tony Blair.
47. *Daily Telegraph* (online edition), 16 October 2014.
48. Cannadine (1993: 10).

49. Memorandum by Capt. R. V. Briscoe, RN (ret.), written at Rome, 8 March 1913, at Balfour's request, Whittingehame MSS 74, quoted in Foster (1981: 127).

50. *Universe Today* (online edition), 22 March 2015.

51. *Guardian* (online edition), 22 March 2016.

52. 'Trend Watch', Merriam-Webster, 22 January 2017 www.merriam-webster.com (accessed 27 December 2017).

53. Trypanis (1955: 18). It subsequently appeared in *The Charioteer: A Quarterly Review of Modern Greek Culture* (New York, 1961).

54. *Independent* (online edition), 21 January 1993.

55. Smedley (1868: 4).

56. Sir John Franklin (1786–1847), naval officer and Arctic explorer.

57. Franklin (1823: 345).

58. *Quarterly Review*, 28 (1823), 389.

59. I find it interesting that one of Kipling's stories turns on something similar: a particular phrase that has embedded itself in a person's mind. In the short story 'Fairy Kist' the shell-shocked Wollin is suspected of murder because his compulsion for planting 'for such as have no gardens' (a phrase that echoes in his mind) places him in proximity to a suspicious death. Demonstrating Wollin's innocence, the doctor also shows that the words come from a story by Mrs Ewing, *Mary's Meadow*, which had been read to him by a nurse when he was hospitalized and which his conscious mind had forgotten. See further Knowles (1986).

Chapter 4

1. Samuel Johnson to James Boswell, May 1781, quoted in *ODQ* (2014: 429).

2. Crystal (2010: 1–3).

3. 'Salt of the earth' in fact goes back a considerable way beyond early modern translations. The *OED* entry for the phrase cites the Lindisfarne Gospels of *c*.950, 'Gee sint salt eorðes', and it is found in Chaucer's *Summoner's Tale*.

4. Hyman (2005: 16).

5. Tony Blair was born in 1953. David Cameron was born in 1966, and it is probable that future incumbents will be younger still. How many more prime ministers, churchgoing or not, will be familiar with the King James Version?

6. Quoted at length in Wells (1987: pp. xi–xii).

7. *Entrepreneur* (online edition), 22 April 2016.

8. *Independent* (online edition), 28 October 2013.

9. Mann (1961: 116).

10. WTNH *Connecticut News* (online edition), 9 August 2015.

11. 'The Two Voices' (1842), in Tennyson (2000: 63).

12. Tennyson (1897: 193). Hallam Tennyson also quoted from the literary editor and biographer James Spedding (1808–81), writing in the *Edinburgh Review* of April 1843: 'In "The Two Voices" we have a history of the agitations, the suggestions and counter-suggestions of a mind sunk in hopeless despondency.'

13. As, for example, the inscription on the Martin Luther King memorial discussed in Chapter 6.

14. For a fuller examination of the history this phrase in the language, see Knowles (2011).

15. *Atlantic* (online edition), 15 November 2011.

16. For another citation from the 'Ten Conservative Principles', see Chapter 6.

17. Alexander Pope, 'An Epistle to Dr Arbuthnot' (1735), quoted in ODQ (2014: 602).

18. See damn, *v.* in OED, draft additions, March 2006.

19. *Washington Post* (online edition), 15 January 2017.

20. Peter Hitchens, *Mail Online*, 22 January 2017.

21. *Daily Telegraph* (online edition), 23 April 2007.

22. Lord Carnarvon, House of Lords, 16 October 1820.

23. James (1981: 369).

24. Lewis (1960: 225).

25. Osborne (1999: 69).

26. See De Retz (1917: i. 82), 'it is more unbecoming a minister to speak foolishly, than act foolishly', and De Retz (1917: ii. 20), 'a man that does not confide in himself, will never confide sincerely in anyone'.

27. Published posthumously as *Mémoires* in 1717. For further details, see Salmon (1969: 1).

28. In English usage, 'defining moment' is likely to be the preferred phrase. OED now treats this as a defined lemma, with evidence recorded from 1967 (see Draft Additions, March 2003, under *defining* adj.).

29. Lord Chesterfield, letter to his son, 25 March 1748; Chesterfield (1774: 260).

30. De Retz is generally quoted in translation in English sources, and translations naturally vary. 'A man who doesn't trust himself can never really trust anyone', which appears on *ThinkExist.com* and other

quotation sites, is represented in Everyman translation (based on an eighteenth-century original) as 'a man that does not confide in himself, will never confide sincerely in anyone' (see De Retz 1917: ii. 20).

31. James Madison, 'Commonplace Book, 1759–1770', Founders Online, US National Archives, <https://founders.archives.gov> (accessed 2 January 2018). See this source for a discussion about the date of the Commonplace Book

32. See Hume (2014: 103). As the editors explain, this is a paraphrase of Hume's dicta that 'there are matters upon which it is certain that the world desires to be deceived' (De Retz 1917: ii. 60), and 'it is more unbecoming a minister to speak foolishly than to act foolishly' (De Retz 1917: ii. 60).

33. Smith (2014: 286).

34. Jenkins (1851: 337–8); 'Joseph C. Yates'.

35. D'Israeli (1818: 285).

36. D'Israeli (1839: 304).

37. Lord Rowton in the Hughenden Papers, 14 December 1878, quoted in Blake (1966: 254). Disraeli's use of the maxim in conversation with Rowton is also noted in Monypenny and Buckle's *Life* of Disraeli (Monypenny and Buckle 1912: 304).

38. For a detailed account of this process, and what it can tell us about methods of pre-Internet quotation searches, see Chapter 2.

39. Watson (1904: 61).

40. Martin Gilbert notes that Masterman had been Under-Secretary of State to Churchill at the Home Office in 1919. See Gilbert (1988: 567). Masterman's admiration for Watson, as compared with 'Imperialist' writers such as W. E. Henley and Kipling, is made explicit in his essay 'After the Reaction' (Masterman 1905: 10–11).

41. Lord Hale, speech on Commonwealth Consultation, House of Lords, 9 May 1973.

42. Henry Campbell-Bannerman, speech in Stirling, 17 January 1905, reported in *Guardian*, 18 January 1905.

Chapter 5

1. William Wordsworth, 'Composed upon Westminster Bridge' (1807), quoted in *ODQ* (2014: 836).

2. *Dundalk Democrat* (online edition), 2 February 2016.

3. Graveside oration, 1 August 2015; Pearse (1962: 137).

4. Theresa May, speech to Conservative Party conference, 7 October 2002.

5. *The Times*, 30 August 2016.

6. Theresa May, speech to Conservative Party conference, 5 October 2016.

7. For example, 'Theresa May Flips her Most Famous Soundbite to Attack Labour as the "Nasty Party"', *Huffington Post* (online edition), 5 October 2016.

8. *Daily Beast* (online edition), 21 December 2015.

9. Harris (1988: 313).

10. It clearly has particular appeal for O'Rourke, who reworked it in a column for the London *Times* of 30 May 2016, explaining why he would be endorsing Hillary Clinton rather than Donald Trump. 'Better the devil you know than the Lord of the Flies on his own 757. Flying to and fro in the earth.'

11. Authorized Version; *ODNB* attributes the phrase to Coverdale.

12. Ruskin (1989: 453).

13. *Cyclopedia of Illustrations* (1911: 672).

14. Debate on the Ministry of Supply Bill, House of Commons, 19 June 1939.

15. *Irish Law Times and Solicitors' Reports*, 74 (1940), 314.

16. For a fuller discussion of the history of 'splendid misery', see Knowles (2010).

17. Ellen Fitzpatrick, quoted in *SABC news* (online edition), 1 November 2016.

18. *New York Times* (online edition), 6 October 2008.

19. Thomas Jefferson, letter to Elbridge Gerry, 13 May 1797, in Jefferson (1854: 171).

20. Abigail Adams, letter to her sister, 16 May 1797, in Adams (1947: 90). See Knowles (2010) for a more detailed consideration of why it was the association with Jefferson rather than the one with Abigail Adams that lasted.

21. It appears in Jefferson (1929).

22. 'Death-Bed Thoughts', in Dunton (1682: 95).

23. Young (1906: ii. 108).

24. Maxwell's own wife was confined in a Dublin asylum; it was not until she died in 1874 that Maxwell and Mary Elizabeth were able to marry.

25. *Law Reports*, Chancery Division, 50 (1880), 816.

26. As a later US president, Warren G. Harding (1865–1923), was to name the first generation of American statesmen.
27. Braddon (1880: p. viii).
28. Dwight David Eisenhower (1890–1969), American general and Republican statesman, President of the United States 1953–61.
29. *Chicago Tribune*, 26 March 1969.

Chapter 6

1. See the entry for Thomas Heywood in *ODNB*.
2. Dickens (1957: 424).
3. Parker (2016: 51–3). Quoting from 'The Culprit', Darrow had altered 'county kerchief' to 'County Sheriff'. He had also altered a line in 'When Hollow Fires Burn Out to Black' (*A Shropshire Lad*) from 'lights are guttering low' as 'lights are fluttering low'. However, he did get a third quotation (also from that poem) right. Looking to any future the two young men might have, he told the judge that 'whether the march begins at the gallows or when the gates of Joliet [Penitentiary] close upon them, there is nothing but the night'.
4. For a detailed categorization of possible types of misquotation, see Regier (2010: 21–44); see also Knowles (2006: pp. i–xvii).
5. Woolf (1964: 116–18).
6. Mortimer (1991: 221).
7. *Guardian* (online edition), 7 February 2011.
8. Motley (1858: 481, concluding words). The *American National Biography* entry for Motley notes of the popularity of this three-volume work that it 'received immediate and popular acclaim (by 1857, 15,000 copies had been sold in London)'.
9. See also further Maciag (2013).
10. Theresa May, speech to the Conservative Party conference, 5 October 2016.
11. See the website of The Russell Kirk Center for Cultural Renewal, <http://www.kirkcenter.org/> (accessed 27 March 2016).
12. Stanlis (1964: 133).
13. Edmund Burke, letter to Sir Hercules Langrishe, 1782; Burke (2014: ix. 634).
14. Edmund Burke, *Reflections on the Revolution in France* (1790); Burke (2014: viii. 72).

15. Tony Blair, on arriving in Belfast for the Northern Irish peace negotiations, 6 April 1998.
16. Mark Durkan, SDLP Member of Parliament for Foyle, addressing the prime minister in the House of Commons debate on the Chilcot Report, 6 July 2016.
17. Quoted in *Mail on Sunday* (online edition), 31 August 2003.
18. *Sun* (online edition), 11 December 2016.
19. Cresswell (2007).
20. 'French Novels', *Edinburgh Review or Critical Journal*, 34 (1820), 372–3.
21. Charles Dickens, 'The Nickleby Proclamation' (1838); Dickens (1982: i. 3).
22. James Joyce, *Ulysses* (1922), quoted in *OED*, pasture *n*.1.c.
23. *Monthly Chronicle; a National Journal of Politics, Literature, Science, and Art*, 7 (1841), 385–405 at 385.
24. *Household Words*, 3 (1851), 160.
25. Leigh Hunt, letter to James T. Fields, 22 June 1859; Hunt (1862: 299). Hunt's hopes for recovery were not realized, as he died in August of that year.
26. Leigh Hunt, letter to James T. Fields, 24 June 1859; Hunt (1862: 300).
27. Meredith (1888: 163).
28. Forster (1872–4: 155). Forster originally wrote that the creation of the Nickleby family would 'open cheerily to their author "fresh fields and pastures new"'. In later editions this was altered to 'fresh woods and pastures new'.
29. *Academy*, 15 April 1893, p. 318.
30. *Saskatoon Star Phoenix* (online edition), 21 January 2017.
31. *Greenville Daily News* (online edition), 21 January 2017.
32. *Folio Weekly* (online edition), 25 January 2017.
33. Email message quoted in Ulrich (2007: p. xiii).
34. Ulrich (1976).
35. Mills (1995).
36. Maggio (1996).
37. Ulrich (2007: p. xiv).
38. Doyle (1993a: 41).
39. Doyle (1993b: 268) and Doyle (2007: 127) respectively.
40. Doyle (1982: 203).
41. Keith Flamer, '11 Monumental Restorations in Washington DC', in *Forbes* (online edition), 30 September 2016.

42. *Washington Post* (online edition), 1 September 2011.
43. The phrase was not coined by King. The website Martin Luther King Jr Online, <www.mlkonline.net> (accessed 28 December 2017), notes that 'the sermon was an adaptation of the 1952 homily "Drum-Major Instincts" by J. Wallace Hamilton, a well-known, liberal, white Methodist preacher'.
44. *Washington Post*, 1 September 2011.
45. Critics quoted included Maya Angelou, the satirist Stephen Colbert, and King's son Martin Luther King III; *Washington Post* (online edition), 12 January 2012.
46. See further Chapter 2.
47. Spurgeon (1858: 74).

Chapter 7

1. Paine (1795: 32).
2. Paine's writings have remained in the public eye, as Paine himself has retained what is seen as a contemporary relevance. As *The American Dictionary of National Biography* (which affords the English-born Paine a place) comments, 'succeeding generations of radicals ... rediscovered him again and again as a symbol of revolutionary internationalism, free thinking, and defiance of existing institutions'.
3. Graham Greene, letter to V. S. Pritchett; Pritchett (1948: 46).
4. Sherry (1989: 442).
5. *Miami Herald* (online edition), 8 July 2016.
6. The text of the speech is printed in its entirety in Schlesinger (1978: 874–5).
7. As in *New York Times*, 5 April 1968.
8. As in *New York Times*, 7 June 1968.
9. Hamilton (1963). The *American National Biography* entry for Hamilton, noting that her writings on the classical world had contributed to the revival in America of the study of classical civilization, also describes how Robert Kennedy 'drew lasting solace from her books after his brother's death'.
10. Beard (2004: 11). Mary Beard comments that 'the quotation itself is the victim of some (maybe constructive) misremembering'.
11. Kissinger (1982: 1210).
12. *Sunday Leader* (Sri Lanka) (online edition), 15 September 2015.

13. Casazza (2003: 197–9).
14. *Reflections with Peter Hennessy*, broadcast 23 August 2016. <http://www.bbc.co.uk/programmes/b07pgvjg> (accessed 28 December 2017).
15. Boswell (1791), 21 July 1763.
16. Prater (1995: 305).
17. Mann (1961: 193).
18. Mann (1961: 194).
19. 'Globalists on the Left and Right Attacking Trump's Victory', 14 November 2016, <*NewsWithViews.com*> (accessed 28 December 2017).
20. Rothrock (2006: 1).
21. Cicero, *In Catilinam* speech 2, ch. 11, quoted in *ODQ* (2014: 219).
22. Caldwell (1965: 565).
23. *Western Journalism* (online edition), 3 February 2015.
24. See *The Cicero Homepage*, <https://sites.la.utexas.edu/cicero/> (accessed 28 December 2017).
25. 'Myths: Did Cicero Say It?', in *The Cicero Homepage*, <https://sites.la.utexas.edu/cicero> (accessed 28 December 2017).
26. 'The Budget Should be Balanced; the Treasury Should be Refilled', in *Quote Investigator*, <www.quoteinvestigator.com> (accessed 28 December 2017). See also *New York Times*, 14 August 1988.
27. Caldwell (1965: 483). Regrettably for Cicero, of course, the agreement of Antonius, or Mark Antony, proves to be theoretical rather than actual.
28. *Life Site* (online edition), 8 July 2016.
29. Pseudonym of Cecil William Mercer (1885–1960).
30. Yates (1945: 263).

Chapter 8

1. *Daily Telegraph* (online edition), 17 January 2017.
2. Noel Coward, diary, 19 March 1955; Coward (1983: 261).
3. *Independent* (online edition), 4 September 2015.
4. The story is recounted by Kenneth Harris in his biography of Attlee. Harris's account makes clear the anger of Churchill, who spoke 'with his face set hard' and 'after an awful pause'. See Harris (1982: 244).
5. *New Statesman and Nation*, 24 April 1954, p. 529.
6. Wilson (1949: 97).
7. Howard Brenton and David Hare, *Brassneck*, in *Plays and Players* (October 1973).

8. Fontaine (1968: 276). Fontaine cites a French source for this story, Jacques Chastenet's *Winston Churchill et l'Angleterre due XXe siècle*.

9. Marr (2008: 17).

10. Green and Laurie (1951: 337).

11. Sandburg (1936: 100).

12. For an example of this discussed earlier, see Gore Vidal and 'good career move', in Chapter 3.

13. Strode (1905).

14. *Computer Dealer News* (online edition), 27 May 2016.

15. Maxtone-Graham (1988).

16. See Garson O'Toole's detailed account, and the subsequent correspondence, at *Quote Investigator* <www.quoteinvestigator.com> (accessed 29 December 2017).

17. Mill (1967: 74).

18. *Times* (Times Digital Archive), 13 August 1936.

19. The US midterm elections of autumn 1951.

20. *New York Times* (online edition), 10 November 1951.

21. According to his obituary in the *New York Times* of 25 April 1991, 'John Roy Carlson was the pen name of the anti-Fascist writer Arthur Derounian'.

22. John Roy Carlson, 'McCarthyism Opposed: Danger to our Democracy Seen not in the Man but in the Movement', *New York Times*, 29 May 1953.

23. Joseph McCarthy's dominance was ended in 1954, following the televising in April 1954 of the US Senate hearings on subversion in the US army. The public exposure of his mode of questioning proved deeply damaging to McCarthy, and he was censured by the Senate in the autumn of that year.

24. Admiral Arthur W. Radford was described in *The American National Biography* as 'the principal "hawk" in the Eisenhower administration'. In 1955 he had urged President Eisenhower to launch an atomic attack on Communist China.

25. For an account of 'the post-World War II revival of interest in Burke and his inauguration as "the father of modern Conservatism"', see Maciag (2013).

26. Lord Birdwood, House of Lords, 4 July 1957.

27. Evelyn Lincoln, letter, 20 August 1962; in Papers of President Kennedy, White House Central Files, 1/20/1961–11/22/1963, US National Archives, <https://catalog.archives.gov> (accessed 2 January 2018).

28. William Safire gives a detailed account in two of his 'On Language' columns in *New York Times*: see Safire (1980, 1981).

29. *Blurb Magazine* (online edition), 1 November 2015.

30. *News OK* (online edition), 20 January 2016.

31. Douglas MacArthur, speech to annual reunion of veterans of the 'Rainbow Division', Washington DC, 14 July 1935; MacArthur (1965: 72–3). The 'Rainbow Division' was the 42nd Division. MacArthur had been its chief of staff in France in the First World War.

32. Douglas MacArthur, speech to cadets at West Point, 12 May 1962; MacArthur (1965: 353).

33. 'Tipperary', in Santayana (1922: 102).

34. McCarthy (1989: 248).

35. Richard Schickel, 'Soldiers on the Screen', *Time* (online edition), 17 November 2001.

36. Lawrence and McGarrahan (2008: 454).

REFERENCES

Further Reading

Recent publications that contribute significantly to the study of quotations include Ruth Finnegan, *Why Do We Quote?* (Finnegan, 2011), Gary Saul Morson, *The Words of Others* (Morson, 2011), and Willis Goth Regier, *Quotology* (Regier, 2010). For online resources focusing on the history of individual quotations, see especially *Quote Investigator: Exploring the Origins of Quotations* (www.quoteinvestigator.com).

Archives

Archival material quoted from the files of Oxford University Press.

Publications

Adams, Abigail (1947). *New Letters of Abigail Adams*, ed. Mary Smith Cranch and Stewart Mitchell. Boston: Houghton Mifflin.

Anglund, Joan Walsh (1968). *A Cup of Sun: A Book of Poems.* London: Collins.

Austermühl, Frank (2014). *The Great American Scaffold: Intertextuality and Identity in American Presidential Discourse.* Amsterdam; Philadelphia: John Benjamins Publishing.

Bamborough, J. B. (2012). 'Introduction', in Thomas C. Faulkner, Nicolas K. Kiessling, and Rhonda L. Blair (eds), *Robert Burton's The Anatomy of Melancholy.* Online edition. Oxford: Oxford University Press, i.

Bartlett, John (1855). *A Collection of Familiar Quotations.* Cambridge, Mass.: J. Bartlett.

Bartlett's Familiar Quotations: a collection of passages, phrases, and proverbs traced to their sources in ancient and modern literature (2012). 18th edn, ed. Geoffrey O'Brien. New York: Little, Brown and Company.

Beard, Mary (2004). 'All Too Sayable', review of Edith Hall, Fiona Macintosh, and Amanda Wrigley (eds), *Dionysus since 69: Greek Tragedy at the Dawn of the Third Millennium* (Oxford University Press, 2004), in *Times Literary Supplement*, 15 October 2004, p. 11.

Bell, Martin (2009). *A Very British Revolution: The Expenses Scandal and how to Save our Democracy*. London: Icon Books.

Benham, William Gurney (1912). *Cassell's Book of Quotations, Proverbs, and Household Words: a collection of quotations from British and American authors, with many thousands of proverbs*. Rev. edn. London: Cassell and Company, Ltd.

Bennett, Alan (2007). *The Uncommon Reader*. London: Faber and Faber.

Blake, Robert (1966). *Disraeli*. London: Eyre and Spottiswoode.

Bohn, Henry George (1881). *A Dictionary of Quotations from the English Poets*. London: George Bell and Sons. Verbatim issue with corrections of original 1867 private printing.

Boswell, James, *Life of Samuel Johnson*. London: printed by Henry Baldwin for Charles Dilly, 1791.

Brabanter, Philippe de (c.2005). *Hybrid Quotations*. Amsterdam: John Benjamins Publishing.

Braddon, Mary Elizabeth (1880). *The Story of Barbara*. 3 vols. London: John and Robert Maxwell.

Bülow, Bernard, Prince von (1931). *Memoirs 1897–1903*, trans. F. A. Voigt. London and New York: Putnam.

Bulwer-Lytton, Edward (2010). *Paul Clifford* (1830). London: Penguin Books.

Burke, Edmund (2014). *The Writings and Speeches of Edmund Burke*, ed. L. G. Mitchell and William B. Todd. 9 vols. Online edition. Oxford: Oxford University Press.

Bysshe, Edward (1702). *The Art of English Poetry: containing i. rules for making verses, ii. a dictionary of rhymes, iii. a collection of the most noble thoughts that are to be found in the best English poets*. London: R. Knaplock.

Caldwell, Taylor (1965). *A Pillar of Iron*. New York: Doubleday.

Cannadine, David (1993). 'Churchill and the Pitfalls of Family Life', in Robert Blake and William Roger Louis (eds), *Churchill*. Oxford: Oxford University Press.

Casazza, Joseph (2003). '"Taming the Savageness of Man": Robert Kennedy, Edith Hamilton, and their Sources', *Classical World*, 96/2: 197–9.

Chesterfield, Lord (1774). *Letters Written by the Right Honourable Philip Dormer Stanhope, Earl of Chesterfield, to his Son*. 2 vols. Dublin: printed by G. Faulkner. Eighteenth Century Collections Online.

Cooper, J. Fenimore (2009). *The Ways of the Hour* (1851). Newcastle-on-Tyne: Cambridge Scholars Publishing.

Cooper, Thomas (1578). *Thesaurus Linguae Romanae & Britannica*. London: Henry Denham. New edn.

Coward, Noël (1983). *The Noël Coward Diaries*, ed. Graham Payn and Sheridan Morley. London: Papermac.

Cresswell, Julia (2007). *The Cat's Pyjamas: The Penguin Book of Clichés*. London: Penguin.

Crystal, David (2010). *Begat: The King James Bible and the English Language*. Oxford: Oxford University Press.

Dallek, Robert (2008). *Harry S. Truman*. New York: Times Books.

De Retz, Jean-Paul-François de Gondi, Cardinal (1917). *Memoirs*, trans. 1723 by Peter Davall; ed. David Ogg. 2 vols. London: J. M. Dent and Sons.

Dickens, Charles (1957). 'Mrs Joseph Porter', in *Sketches by Boz: Illustrative of Every-Day Life and Every-Day People* (1836). London: Oxford University Press.

Dickens, Charles (1982). 'The Nickleby Proclamation', in *The Life and Adventures of Nicholas Nickleby* (reproduced in facsimile from the original monthly parts of 1838–9). 2 vols. London: Scolar Press.

D'Israeli, Isaac (1818). *The Literary Character, Illustrated by the History of Men of Genius*. London: John Murray.

D'Israeli, Isaac (1839). *The Literary Character, Illustrated by the History of Men of Genius*. 5th edn. London: John Murray.

Doyle, Arthur Conan (1982). 'The Fate of the Evangeline' (1885), in *Uncollected Stories*, ed. John Michael Gibson and Richard Lancelyn Green. London: Secker and Warburg.

Doyle, Arthur Conan (1993a). *The Sign of the Four* (1890), ed. Christopher Roden. Oxford: Oxford University Press.

Doyle, Arthur Conan (1993b). 'The Beryl Coronet', in *The Adventures of Sherlock Holmes* (1892), ed. Richard Lancelyn Green. Oxford: Oxford University Press.

Doyle, Arthur Conan (2007). 'The Adventure of the Bruce-Partington Plans', in *His Last Bow [1917] and The Case-Book of Sherlock Holmes*. London: Penguin Books.

Dunbar, Paul Laurence (1997). 'Sympathy', from *Lyrics of the Hearthside* (New York: Dodd, Mead & Co., 1899), in *Paul Laurence Dunbar Selected Poems*, ed. Glenn Mott. New York: Dover Publications.

Dunton, John (1682). *The House of Weeping: Or Mans Last Progress to his Long Home*. London: printed for John Dunton.

Finnegan, Ruth H. (2011). *Why Do We Quote? The Culture and History of Quotations*. Cambridge: Open Book Publishers.

Fontaine, André (1968). *History of the Cold War: From the October Revolution to the Korean War, 1917–1950*, trans. D. D. Paige. London: Secker and Warburg.

Forster, John (1872–4). *The Life of Charles Dickens*. 3 vols. London: Chapman and Hall.

Foster, R. F. (1981). *Lord Randolph Churchill: A Political Life*. Oxford: Clarendon Press.

Franklin, John (1823). *Narrative of a Journey to the Shores of the Polar Sea in the Years 1819, 20, 21, and 22*. London: John Murray.

Friswell, James (1865). *Familiar Words: An Index Verborum or Quotation Handbook*. London: Sampson Low, Son, and Marston.

Garber, Marjorie (2003). *Quotation Marks*. New York and London: Routledge.

Gent, L. C. (1852). *The Book of Familiar Quotations*. London: Whitaker.

Gilbert, Martin (1988). *'Never Despair': Winston S. Churchill 1945–1965*. London: Heinemann.

Green, Abel, and Laurie, Joe, Jr (1951). *Show Biz from Vaude to Video*. New York: Henry Holt.

Hamilton, Edith (1963). *The Greek Way*. New York: New American Library. (First published, London: Dent, 1930.)

Hancher Michael (2003). 'Familiar Quotations', *Harvard Library Bulletin*, 14/2: 13–47.

Harris, Kenneth (1982). *Attlee*. London: Weidenfeld & Nicolson.

Harris, Thomas (1988). *The Silence of the Lambs*. London: Heinemann.

Hastings, Max (1979). *Bomber Command*. London: Michael Joseph.

Hearne, Thomas (1869). *Reliquiae Hernianae: The Remains of Thomas Hearne, MA*, ed. Philip Bliss. 2nd edn. 3 vols. London: John Russell Smith.

Higgins, Charlotte (2013). *Under Another Sky: Journeys in Roman Britain*. London: Vintage.

Hoyt, Jehiel Keeler and Ward, Anna Lydia (1882). *The Cyclopædia of Practical Quotations, English and Latin*. New York: I. K. Funk & Co.

Hoyt's New Cyclopedia of Practical Quotations: drawn from the speech and literature of all nations, ancient and modern, classic and popular, in English and foreign text (1923). Ed. Kate Louise Roberts. New York: Funk & Wagnalls.

Hume, David (2014). *A Treatise of Human Nature* (1739–40), in *The Clarendon Edition of the Works of David Hume*, ed. David Fate Norton and Mary J. Norton. Online edition. Oxford: Oxford University Press, i.

Hunt, Leigh (1862). *The Correspondence of Leigh Hunt, Edited by his Eldest Son*. 2 vols. London: Smith, Elder and Co.

Hyman, Peter (2005). *1 Out of 10*. London: Vintage.

James, Henry (1981). *The Portrait of a Lady* (1880–1). Oxford: Oxford University Press.

Jay, Antony (1996) (ed.). *The Oxford Dictionary of Political Quotations*. Oxford: Oxford University Press.

Jefferson, Thomas (1829). *The Memoirs, Correspondence, and Private Papers of Thomas Jefferson*, ed. Thomas Jefferson Randolph. 3 vols. London: Ibotson and Palmer.

Jefferson, Thomas (1854). *The Writings of Thomas Jefferson: Being His Autobiography, Correspondence, Reports, Messages, Addresses, and Other Writings, Official and Private*. 9 vols, 1853–4. Washington: Taylor & Maury.

Jenkins, John S. (1851). *Lives of the Governors of the State of New York*. New York: Derby and Miller.

Kissinger, Henry (1982). *Years of Upheaval*. London: Weidenfeld & Nicolson and Michael Joseph.

Knowles, Elizabeth (1986). 'Seven Portugal Onions: A Note on Kipling's Reading', *Kipling Journal* (December), 43–8.

Knowles, Elizabeth (2006). *What They Didn't Say: A Book of Misquotations*. Oxford: Oxford University Press.

Knowles, Elizabeth (2009). 'Dictionaries of Quotations', in A. P. Cowie (ed.), *The Oxford History of English Lexicography*. 2 vols. Oxford: Clarendon Press, ii. 245–68.

Knowles, Elizabeth (2010). '"A Hackneyed Phrase": *Splendid Misery* as a Case Study in Quotation Usage' in Michael Adams (ed.), *'Cunning Passages, Contrived Corridors': Unexpected Essays in the History of Lexicography*. Milan: Polimetrica.

Knowles, Elizabeth (2011). 'Chaos and Old Night: A Case Study in Quotation Usage', in Olga Timofeeva and Tanja Säily (eds), *Words in Dictionaries and History: Essays in Honour of R. W. McConchie*. Amsterdam; Philadelphia: John Benjamins Publishing, 91–108.

Lawrence, John Shelton, and McGarrahan, John G. (2008). 'Operation Restore Honor in *Black Hawk Down*', in Peter C. Rollins and John E. O'Connor (eds), *Why We Fought: America's Wars in Film and History*. Lexington: University of Kentucky Press, 431–57.

Lewis, C. S. (1960). *Studies in Words*. Cambridge: Cambridge University Press.

MacArthur, Douglas (1965). *A Soldier Speaks: Public Papers and Speeches of General of the Army Douglas MacArthur*. New York: Frederick A. Praeger.

McCarthy, Cormac (1989). *Blood Meridian*. London: Picador.

Maciag, Drew (2013). *Edmund Burke in America: The Contested Career of the Father of Modern Conservatism*. Ithaca, NY: Cornell University Press.

Maggio, Rosalie (1996) (ed.). *The New Beacon Book of Quotations by Women*. Boston: Beacon Press.

Malvern, Sue (2004). '"For King and Country": Frampton's Edith Cavell (1915–20) and the Writing of Gender in Memorials to the Great War', in David J. Getsy (ed.), *Sculpture and the Pursuit of a Modern Ideal in Britain, c.1880–1930*. Aldershot: Ashgate Publishing.

Mann, Thomas (1961). *The Story of a Novel: The Genesis of Doctor Faustus*, trans. from the German by Richard Winson and Clara Winson. New York: Alfred A. Knopf. (Published in German in 1949 as *Die Entstehung Des Doktor Faustus*. Amsterdam: Bermann-Fischer Verlag.)

Marr, Andrew (2008). *A History of Modern Britain*. London: Pan Macmillan.

Masterman, C. F. G. (1905). 'After the Reaction', in *In Peril of Change: Essays Written in a Time of Tranquillity*. London: T. Fisher-Unwin.

Maud, Constance Elizabeth (1918). 'César Franck: The War Musician of Unconquerable France', *Nineteenth Century and After* (November), 921–33.

Maxtone-Graham, John (1988). *Safe Return Doubtful: The Heroic Age of Polar Exploration*. New York: Patrick Stephens.

Mencken, H. L. (1942). *A New Dictionary of Quotations on Historical Principles from Ancient and Modern Sources*. New York: Alfred A. Knopf.

Meredith, Edmund Allen (1888). 'Current Misquotations', *Andover Review*, 10 (August), 156–69.

Mill, John Stuart (1867). *Inaugural Address Delivered to the University of St Andrews, Feb. 1st 1867*. London: Longmans, Green, Reader, and Dyer.

Mills, Kay (1995). *From Pocahontas to Power Suits: Everything you Need to Know about Women's History in America*. New York: Plume.

Monypenny, W. F., and Buckle, G. E. (1912). *The Life of Benjamin Disraeli, Earl of Beaconsfield*. ii. London: John Murray.

Moon, Rosamund (1989). 'Objective or Objectionable? Ideological Aspects of Dictionaries', *English Language Research Journal*, 3: 59–91.

Morris, Lewis (1890). *The Works of Lewis Morris*. London: Kegan Paul, Trench, Trübner & Co.

Morson, Gary Saul (2011). *The Words of Others: From Quotations to Culture*. New Haven and London: Yale University Press.

Mortimer, John (1987). 'Rumpole and the Official Secret', in *The Second Rumpole Omnibus*. London: Viking, 511–48.

Mortimer, John (1991). 'Rumpole for the Prosecution', in *Rumpole à la Carte*. London: Viking, 204–46.

Motley, John Lothrop (1858). *The Rise of the Dutch Republic*. 3 vols. London: George Routledge.

Noonan, Peggy (1990). *What I Saw at the Revolution: A Political Life in the Reagan Era*. New York: Random House.

Osborne, John (1999). *Looking Back: Never Explain, Never Apologise*. London: Faber and Faber.

The Oxford Dictionary of Quotations (2014). 8th edn, ed. Elizabeth Knowles. Oxford: Oxford University Press.

Paine, Thomas (1905). *Dissertation on First Principles of Government*. Paris. Eighteenth Century Collections Online <http://find.galegroup.com/ ecco> (accessed 3 January 2018).

Parker, Peter (2016). *Housman Country: Into the Heart of England*. Online edition. London: Little, Brown.

Pearse, Pàdraic H. (1962). *Political Writings and Speeches*. Dublin: Talbot Press.

Petrey, Sandy (1980). *History in the Text: 'Quatrevingt-treize' and the French Revolution*. Amsterdam: John Benjamins Publishing.

Piper, David (1964). *The Companion Guide to London*. London: Collins.

Plimpton, George (1998) (ed.). *Truman Capote: In which Various Friends, Enemies, Acquaintances, and Detractors Recall his Turbulent Career*. New York: Doubleday.

Prater, Donald (1995). *Thomas Mann: A Life*. Oxford: Oxford University Press.

Pritchett, V. S. (1948). *Why Do I Write? An Exchange of Views between Elizabeth Bowen, Graham Greene, and V. S. Pritchett*, with a preface by V. S. Pritchett. London: P. Marshall.

Ratcliffe, Susan (2011) (ed.). *The Oxford Treasury of Sayings and Quotations*. 4th edn. Oxford: Oxford University Press.

Rees, Nigel (1997). *Cassell Companion to Quotations*. London: Cassell.

Rees, Nigel (2006). *Brewer's Famous Quotations*. London: Chambers Harrap Publishers.

Regier, Willis Goth (2010). *Quotology*. Lincoln, NA, and London: University of Nebraska Press.

Rothrock, James (2006). *Divided We Fall: How Disunity Leads to Defeat*. Bloomington, IN: AuthorHouse.

Ruffin, Edmund (1857). 'Extracts from the Diary of Edmund Ruffin', cited in *William and Mary Quarterly*, 23 (1915), 240–58.

Ruskin, John (1989). *Praeterita: The Autobiography of John Ruskin* (1885–9), ed. Kenneth Clark. Oxford: Oxford University Press.

Safire, William (1980). 'On Language', column in *New York Times*, 9 March 1980.

Safire, William (1981). 'On Language', column in *New York Times*, 5 April 1981.

Salmon, J. H. M. (1969). *Cardinal de Retz: The Anatomy of a Conspirator*. London: Weidenfeld and Nicolson.

Sandburg, Carl (1936). *The People, Yes*. New York: Harcourt, Brace and Co.

Santayana, George (1922). *Soliloquies in England and Later Soliloquies*. London: Constable.

Schlesinger, Arthur M., Jr (1978). *Robert Kennedy and his Times*. Boston: Houghton Mifflin.

Shapiro, Fred R. (2006). *The Yale Book of Quotations*. New Haven, Conn.: Yale University Press.

Shaw, George Bernard (1995). Preface to *St Joan* (1924), in *Bernard Shaw: The Complete Prefaces*, ii. *1914–1929*, ed. Dan H. Laurence and Daniel J. Leary. London: Allen Lane, The Penguin Press.

Sherry, Norman (1989). *The Life of Graham Greene*. London: Penguin Books.

Smedley, Menella Bute (1868). 'A North Pole Story', in [Menella Bute Smedley and Elizabeth Anna Hart], *Poems Written for a Child by Two Friends*. London: Strahan, 1–8.

Smith, Adam (2014). *The Theory of Moral Sentiments* (1790), in D. D. Raphael and A. L. Macfie (eds), *The Glasgow Edition of the Works and Correspondence of Adam Smith*. Online edition. Oxford: Oxford University Press.

Spurgeon, C. H. (1858). *Gems from Spurgeon: Or, Extracts from the Note-Book of A Non-Professional Reporter*. London: Partridge.

Squire, J. C. (1921). 'Quotations', *Living Age*, 15 January, p. 167.

Stanlis, Peter J. (1964) (ed.). *The Relevance of Edmund Burke: Edmund Burke Symposium*. Georgetown: Georgetown University and Edmund Burke Society of America.

Strode, Muriel (1905). *My Little Book of Prayer*. Chicago: Open Court Publishing.

Tennyson, Alfred (2000). *Alfred Tennyson*, ed. Adam Roberts. Oxford: Oxford University Press.

Tennyson, Hallam (1897). *Alfred, Lord Tennyson: A Memoir*. 2 vols. London: Macmillan.

Thackeray, William Makepeace (1994). *The History of Pendennis* (1848–50), ed. John Sutherland. Oxford: Oxford University Press.

Trypanis, C. A. (1955). 'Picture of the Nativity in the Church of Krena in Chios', in *Pedasus: Twenty-Four Poems*. Reading, Berks: printed in the School of Art, University of Reading.

Ulrich, Laurel Thatcher (1976). 'Vertuous Women Found: New England Ministerial Literature, 1668–1735', *American Quarterly* 28 (Spring), 20–40.

Ulrich, Laurel Thatcher (2007). *Well-Behaved Women Seldom Make History*. New York: Alfred A. Knopf.

Watson, William (1904). *For England: Verses Written in Estrangement*. London and New York: John Lane, The Bodley Head.

Wells, Stanley (1987). *An Oxford Anthology of Shakespeare*, selected and introduced by Stanley Wells. Oxford: Clarendon Press.

Wilson, Angus (1949). *The Wrong Set: And Other Stories*. London: Secker and Warburg.

Wood, Anthony à (1721). *Athenæ Oxoniensis: an exact history of all the writers and bishops who have had their education in the most antient and famous university of Oxford, from the fifteenth year of King Henry the Seventh, A.D. 1500, to the author's death in 1695*. 2nd edn. 2 vols. London: printed for R. Knaplock, D. Midwinter, and J. Tonson.

Woolf, Leonard (1964). *Beginning Again: An Autobiography of the Years 1911 to 1918*. London: Hogarth Press.

Woolf, Virginia (1992). *The Years* (1937), ed. Hermione Lee. Oxford: Oxford University Press.

Yates, Dornford (1945). *The House that Berry Built*. London: Ward, Lock & Co.

Young, Edward (1906). 'Love of Fame' (1752), in *Poetical Works of Edward Young*, ed. J. Mitford. 2 vols. London: George Bell & Sons.

PICTURE ACKNOWLEDGEMENTS

1 Keystone Pictures USA / Alamy Stock Photo
2 Clive Limpkin/Daily Mail/REX/Shutterstock
3 Google Books Ngram Viewer http://books.google.com/ngram
4 The Bodleian Library, University of Oxford, (OC) 280 j.947, folio B4
5 Courtesy Quote Investigator
6 Reprinted by permission of the Secretary to the Delegates of Oxford University Press
7 Oxford Reference Online/Oxford Dictionary of Quotations, 8E. By permission of Oxford University Press
8 Andrew Burton/Getty Images
9 Xavier Laine/Getty Images
10 Graham Prentice / Alamy Stock Photo
11 Simon Periton, *The Alchemical Tree*, Installation view, Radcliffe University Quarter, Oxford, 2015 © Simon Periton, courtesy Sadie Coles HQ, London. Photography: © Edmund Blok
12 Courtesy of Goss & Crested China Ltd.
13 © Bank of England 2017
14 Simon Weir / Alamy Stock Photo
15 Kevin Weaver/Getty Images
16 ©Radio Times / Immediate Media
17 Brandon Bourdages © 123RF.com
18 Courtesy of www.paulsteucke.com

INDEX OF QUOTATIONS

INDEX OF NAMES